If you have wondered what lies behind so many extraordinary testimonies of healings coming out of Redding, California, the answer is found in this unusual book. Caution: it is essential reading to those who desire intimacy with God *and* are willing to pay any price, including losing respectability, to have it. If it is intimacy with God you truly want, this is the book for you. Bill Johnson has written a no-nonsense, moving, and thrilling book—one of the best I have read in years.

—Dr. R. T. Kendall
Former pastor, Westminster Chapel, London, England
Best-selling author of *Total Forgiveness*

Face to Face With God, Bill Johnson's newest book, is a must-read, especially for those who have been powerfully touched by the anointing for healing that has come upon Bill's life and who wonder how he received such a strong anointing for healing. This book reveals not only how he has transformed his mind, resulting in spiritual renewal, including power to heal the sick, but it also reveals some of the personal journey that led him to this change in thinking. Do not think this is going to be a how-to book; rather, it is more like a light that points us to the safety of grace and warns us of the rocks of religion, the shallow water of striving, and the waste lands of works. There is gold in these pages. The secret behind Bill's wealth of revelational teaching is relationship. He is one who has not ignored grace's invitation to meeting face-to-face. If you are looking for a book strongly based upon the Bible, Christ-centered for direction, and Spirit-dependent to follow that direction, then you have found it in *Face to Face With God*.

—Randy Clark
Founder, Global Awakening
Author, *God Can Use Little Ol' Me*

Face to Face With God is a book that helps to draw a map to the paths that teach you how to have the quality of relationship with God you have always dreamed of. Starting with Bill's own candid stories of personal desperation for more of God, he takes us on a journey that will not only define spiritual hunger but will also explain how God satisfies a believer with His very face. So many people write about favor, face-to-face relationship with Jesus, and even joy, but I love Bill's way of processing, which is a rare gift filled with understanding for our generation to make the deep but easy connection that God longs for. I ate his perspective up from beginning to end and have to say that it takes a rare book like this to redirect my whole way of approaching my personal devotional times and so affirm God's nature to me. I very rarely write a review for a book that affected me so personally, so it is my pleasure to highly recommend this one especially to leaders and people of influence.

—SHAWN BOLZ
Senior Pastor, Expression58 Ministries
Author, *The Throne Room Company* and
Keys to Heaven's Economy

FACE *to* FACE *with*

BILL JOHNSON

Charisma
HOUSE
A STRANG COMPANY

Most STRANG COMMUNICATIONS/CHARISMA HOUSE/SILOAM/FRONTLINE/
REALMS/EXCEL BOOKS products are available at special quantity discounts for bulk pur-
chase for sales promotions, premiums, fund-raising, and educational needs. For details,
write Strang Communications/Charisma House/Siloam/FrontLine/Realms/Excel
Books, 600 Rinehart Road, Lake Mary, Florida 32746, or telephone (407) 333-0600.

FACE TO FACE WITH GOD by Bill Johnson
Published by Charisma House
A Strang Company
600 Rinehart Road
Lake Mary, Florida 32746
www.charismahouse.com

Unless otherwise noted, all Scripture quotations are from the New American Standard
Bible–Updated Edition, Copyright © 1960, 1962, 1963, 1968, 1971, 1972, 1973, 1975,
1977, 1995 by The Lockman Foundation. Used by permission. (www.Lockman.org)

Scripture quotations marked NKJV are from the New King James Version of the Bible.
Copyright © 1979, 1980, 1982 by Thomas Nelson, Inc., publishers. Used by permission.

Scripture quotations marked KJV are from the King James Version of the Bible.

Scripture quotations marked NIV are from the Holy Bible, New International Version.
Copyright © 1973, 1978, 1984, International Bible Society. Used by permission.

Scripture quotations marked THE MESSAGE are from *The Message: The Bible in
Contemporary English*, copyright © 1993, 1994, 1995, 1996, 2000, 2001, 2002. Used
by permission of NavPress Publishing Group.

Cover Design: Bill Johnson, Executive Design Director, Strang Communications

Library of Congress Cataloging-in-Publication Data

Johnson, Bill, 1951-
Face to face with God / by Bill Johnson.
p. cm.
Includes bibliographical references.
ISBN 978-1-59979-070-1
1. Spirituality. I. Title.
BV4501.3.J6325 2007
248.4--dc22
2007024767

First Edition
08 09 10 11 12 — 10 9 8 7 6 5 4 3
Printed in the United States of America

I dedicate this book to my wonderful wife, Beni. She is my best friend, my wife and lover, and the mother of our three amazing children. Beni illustrates the message of this book more than anyone I know, and she is a great inspiration to me. On top of that, she is a sign and a wonder, for she is a *happy intercessor.*

ACKNOWLEDGMENTS

I want to give special thanks to Dann Farrelly for his continual help and counsel in all my writing. Dann, I owe you big time.

Special thanks to Allison Armerding for helping me "in the last mile." Allison, you did good, again.

Pam, thanks for your editing. Special thanks for doing so while on your vacation.

Thanks to Anne Kalvestrand for helping with research for chapter 7.

Special thanks to Mary Walker (Jodi, too) for helping me complete this project—you're amazing!

CONTENTS

*B*efore Don Miller witnessed a jazz musician playing his instrument with his eyes closed, totally oblivious to any audience, he never liked jazz music. He felt like jazz music "never resolved." He learned something that day as he watched the musician transported by his music to another place, and he concludes: "Sometimes you have to watch somebody love something before you can love it yourself. It's as if they are showing you the way." He had the same feelings about God "because God didn't resolve" (*Blue Like Jazz*, Don Miller).

For me, Bill Johnson is the quintessential model of this unknown musician of Miller's observation. Unlike many of our day who insist on "resolving" God and all of the difficulties He has created for theologians and who insist on needing "pat answers," Bill Johnson plows full speed ahead into the mounds of unresolved issues with questions—sometimes unanswered—and insights that are stunning in their simplicity. Bill's ministry embraces paradox as though it is the most normal thing in the world. He refuses to allow us to embrace a way of thinking that may on the one hand give us an out with a construct that justifies unscriptural conclusions, while on the other hand he shows us with classic simplicity how those paradigms undermine the goodness of God and the practical examples of Jesus Christ in the New Testament.

Often in his teaching ministry Bill will make a statement without "resolving" it and then watch in his classic amusing stance as we all wrestle with the "I've-never-seen-that-before" statement. He will then enlarge upon the previous "unresolved" statement several times and literally talk to himself about how powerful the thought he just shared with us was. His teaching entices you to pursue a way of thinking that is often foreign to traditional teachers, and it whets your appetite for something you always knew was there.

"Sometimes you have to watch somebody love something before you can love it yourself. It's as if they are showing you the way." Face to Face With God is both testimonial and biographical; it is historical and utterly theological. It is the needed narrative that will enable the church to enter into a wholly plausible realm that has always existed for us. Watching Bill Johnson love the presence of God awakens in many of us the slumbering desire to do the same thing. His heroes are those men and women who pursued and are pursuing passionately the presence of God. His message of the power of God is absolutely essential for this season we face. May it be said of us in the twenty-first century as it was of them in the first-century church: "They were amazed and began to recognize them as having been with Jesus."

—BISHOP JOSEPH L. GARLINGTON SR.
Senior Pastor, Covenant Church of Pittsburgh
Presiding Bishop, Reconciliation Ministries International

CHAPTER I

THE JOURNEY
BEGINS

he air is pregnant with possibility—can you feel it? Heaven itself is longing to invade the natural realm. Darkness may cover the earth, but God's glory upon His people is becoming more and more realized, bringing hope to the most hopeless situations.

God is opening up His treasure house of truth and releasing it all over mankind in remarkable ways. The apostle Paul's prayer is being answered before our eyes: I give "thanks for you, while making mention of you in my prayers; that the God of our Lord Jesus Christ, the Father of glory, may give to you the spirit of wisdom and of revelation in the knowledge of Him" (Ephesians 1:16–17, NKJV). Like birth pangs signaling the time of delivery, things are being released in revelation knowledge that have been preserved through the ages for this particular hour. In other words, this exponential increase in wisdom and revelation is being precipitated by the day that God is releasing in our time in history. I'm not talking about new books of the Bible or other holy writings. I'm talking about the Holy Spirit unlocking the very Scriptures we hold in our hands.

And what is this day that God is unveiling? It is a day of divine encounters, at least for those who will *pursue* what this revelation is making available. The spirit of wisdom and revelation is not given to make us smarter but to make us more aware of unseen realities. The purpose of this spirit or anointing is to give us wisdom and revelation *in the knowledge of Him*. It works not merely to increase our understanding of kingdom principles but also to reveal the King Himself. Presence always wins out over principles. When we encounter His divine presence, transformation occurs that goes beyond the reach of merely good ideas—this is transformation that first takes place *within us* that we might cause transformation around us.

THE DESIRE IS A GIFT FROM GOD

The heart to seek God is birthed in us by God Himself. Like all desires, it is not something that can be legislated or forced, but rather it grows within us as we become exposed to God's nature. He creates an appetite in us for Himself by lavishing us with the reality of His goodness—His irresistible glory. God's love for people is beyond comprehension and imagination. He is for us, not against us. God is good 100 percent of the time. These realities burn deeply into the hearts of all who simply take the time to behold Him.

Paul describes this place of beholding as the absolute center of the new covenant we have been brought into, the place where "we all, with unveiled face, beholding as in a mirror the glory of the Lord, are being transformed into the same image from glory to glory, just as by the Spirit of the Lord" (2 Corinthians 3:18, NKJV). The impulse that drives the life of the believer isn't the need to perform for God but to commune with Him. Only when we perceive the face of the One in whose image we were made do we come to know who we are and the One for whom we were made. And because of who He is, to behold

The degree to which we perceive the face of God corresponds directly to the degree of our yieldedness to the transforming work of the Holy Spirit.

Him and remain unchanged is impossible. As He infects us with His presence, we are drawn into an ongoing mission by the One who longs for us. This mission is simply the mission to become more and more fit to see Him in His fullness.

And the truth is that the degree to which we perceive the face of God corresponds directly to the degree of our yieldedness to the transforming work of the Holy Spirit into the image of Christ. The question for every believer is whether we will be satisfied with only a partial transformation or whether we will be so captivated by who He is that we will allow Him to kill everything in us that would inhibit us from becoming a mature manifestation of Christ.

This quest for His face is the ultimate quest. But to embrace the quest for the face of God, one must be ready to die. Thus, this quest is not a journey for the faint of heart. It is far too costly to pursue from mere curiosity.

Still, I hesitate to warn of the cost of fully seeking His face—not because a price doesn't exist; it costs everything. I hesitate because the reality is that what a person gets in return makes the price we pay embarrassingly small by comparison.

The bottom line is that we give all of ourselves to obtain all of Him. There's never been a better deal. When we go through with the exchange, we find that what used to matter doesn't anymore. Life without passion gives way to a life of reckless abandon. Not only does everything in our lives that is inconsistent with the kingdom of God start to die the moment we encounter Him, but the superior, supernatural reality of His kingdom starts to come alive in us. It is not possible to encounter One so overwhelming and maintain the status quo.

This journey is so sacred, so all-consuming, that very few respond to its call. While the seeds of this quest are found in the heart of every man, woman, and child, most seem to be numb to its existence. Many things work to stifle the desire in us to seek the face of the One in whose image we were created. Whether we are overwhelmed by the prevailing winds of secular reasoning or the pain of religious disappointment,[1] such forces cause us to abandon the ultimate quest and give in to the other impulse that has infected man since the Fall—the impulse to hide from God.

Still, the ultimate quest is quite doable and within reach. It is so all-inclusive that the smallest child may come. Every other journey and every other ambition pale in comparison. One might say this one challenge adds meaning and definition to all of life's other pursuits. Those who respond to the invitation find little else to live for. Those who say no spend their lives looking for an adequate replacement. And there is none to be found, anywhere.

MY ASSIGNMENT

Christian leaders in particular have their attention directed toward perceiving what God is revealing for the moment, and they work hard to articulate that revelation in the best way. Whether it's in preaching, in the lyrics of a song, or in a book, we are all attempting to capture that which is divine and release it upon the earth. That's my purpose in this book.

Much of the content of this book was first introduced to our church family around 2002. Preaching it scared me, in all the right ways. This was the only time in my life where I trembled for days following the preaching of a message. However, at the time I was not burdened to release this message in writing, which has been the case with every other book I've written. At the same time, it became my whole life, the life that I have purposed to live, a life devoted to discovering and hosting the presence of God. Pursuing this goal has been costly, but that did not prevent it from becoming more and more fixed in me as my sole reason to be alive. In recent months God has made it clear that the message I have been trying to live is now a message I need to write about.

The quest for deep encounters with God started the moment I said yes to His call on my life. I wasn't called to ministry or to accomplish some great feat in His name. I was called to God Himself. My moment happened one Sunday in 1971 when my dad, who was also my pastor, taught a message from Ezekiel 44 about the greatest honor given to mankind—our ministry to the Lord Himself in thanksgiving, praise, and worship. He taught us that there was a difference between our ministry to God and our ministry to people. There was no doubt that our ministry to God was the most important responsibility of all, and it was available to every believer.

As I heard him teach the Word, I was stirred beyond anything I had ever felt before. While it was not the type of message that one would usually think needed an altar call, I had to respond. From the pew where I sat, I bowed my head and said, "Heavenly Father, I give You the rest of my life to teach me this one thing." To say I was moved was a great understatement. I had already given my life to Christ, in a way where I held nothing back. But I was now saying that in my surrender to Christ I had one specific agenda that outweighed every other—my ministry to the Lord Himself.

It quickly became apparent that this call to worship was not about music, instruments, choirs, or worship teams. Neither was it about using singing to warm up people for the sermon. In this ministry to God, as far as the role of music was concerned, not even the great songs written *about* Him were appropriate. To suit this ministry, I needed songs I could sing *to* Him. It was all about ministering directly to the Lord in His actual presence.

The Lord responded quickly to my lifestyle of abandonment to His presence by confirming, through unfolding revelation, that this was indeed the purpose for which He had made and redeemed me. Scripture is saturated with the theme that we were made for a relationship that allows us to know by experience the supernatural God who created us, and it soon became evident to me that the encounters that God had with people in the Bible were not reserved only for those of that era. Encounters of that magnitude actually started to look possible, even probable again. While I never thought I qualified for anything extraordinary, I knew that He loved me, and I in turn was increasingly hungry for Him.

THE JOURNEY ACCELERATES

I have traveled to many cities where God was visiting in unusual and notable ways in my personal quest for increased power and anointing in my life. Some of my brothers and sisters belittle such pursuits, saying, "Signs and wonders are supposed to follow you, not you follow them." My perspective is a bit different: *If they're not following you, follow them until they follow you.* God has used my experiences in such places to set me up for life-changing encounters at home.

After one such trip in 1995, I began to cry out to God day and night for about eight months. My prayer was, "God, I want more of You at any cost! I will pay any price!" Then, one night in October, God came in answer to my prayer, but not in a way I had expected.

I went from being in a dead sleep to being wide-awake in a moment. Unexplainable power began to pulsate through my body. It was as if I had been plugged into a wall socket with a thousand volts of electricity flowing through my body. An extremely powerful being seemed to have entered the room, and I could not function in His presence. My arms and legs shot out in silent explosions as this power was released through my hands and feet. The more I tried to stop it, the worse it got. I soon discovered that this was not a wrestling match I was going to win. I heard no voice, nor did I have any visions. This was the most overwhelming experience of my life. It was raw power. It was God. He had come in response to the prayer I had been praying.

Now, the evening preceding this encounter had been glorious. Our church had been having a series of meetings with a good friend and prophet, Dick Joyce, and had enjoyed an outstanding time of God's presence and power manifested in the lives of His people. During the ministry time, a friend of mine had had a hard time receiving from God, and I had felt I had a word to give him from God. I told him that God was going to visit him and touch him in a powerful way and that it could happen at any time of the day or night—perhaps two in the afternoon or even *three in the morning*. It would come as a surprise, I told him.

After the great meeting, we finally got to bed around 1:00 a.m. When I was awakened by the power of God, I glanced at the clock and saw that it was exactly 3:00 a.m. I spoke out loud to the Lord, "You set me up!" God had set me up with the prophecy I had given to my friend.

Several times throughout the ten years before this I had experienced the same kind of power in the middle of the night, but only in my legs and with much less intensity. I did not know it was God. I had always thought something was wrong with my body. I would get out of bed and eat a banana, thinking the potassium might help. When that did not work, I would take an anti-inflammatory drug, thinking that might bring relief. That never helped either. This time, at 3:00 a.m., I knew what it was. I felt like Samuel who had been going to the prophet Eli, asking, "Did you call me?" I lay there with the realization that for the previous ten years God had been calling me to something new, something higher. This time He had my full attention—I was unable to move. I understood that, at least in part, this was the "more" that I had been asking for.

I had been asking God to give me more of Him at any cost. I wasn't sure of the correct way to pray, nor did I understand the theology behind my request because I knew He already dwelt in me as a result of my conversion. All I knew was I was hungry for God. There were times I even woke myself in the night because I was asking for more in my sleep. (Some of the most important things that happen to us are the most difficult to explain to others, yet they are undeniably from God. The person having the encounter knows, and that's what matters most.)

Here it was, 3:00 a.m., and it was my moment. But it didn't come in the way I expected—although I couldn't have told you what I expected. He had come to me on a mission. I was His target. It was a glorious experience, because it was Him. But it was not a very pleasant one. It was not gratifying in any natural sense. At first I was embarrassed. I even felt my face turn red, even though I was the only one who knew I was in that condition. As I lay there, I had a mental picture of myself standing before my congregation, teaching from God's Word as I loved to do, but with my arms and legs flailing about as though I had serious physical and emotional problems. Then I saw myself walking down the main street of our town in front of my favorite restaurant in the same condition. I didn't know anyone who would believe that this was from God.

But then I recalled Jacob and his encounter with the angel of the Lord, where he wrestled with Him throughout the night. He limped for the rest of his life after his meeting with God. And then there was Mary, the mother of Jesus. She had an experience with God that not even her fiancé believed was true. It took a visit from an angel to help him change his mind. As a result, she bore the Christ child—although she bore a stigma for the remainder of her days as the mother of an illegitimate child. As I considered these stories, something became clear: from Earth's perspective, the favor of God sometimes looks different than from heaven's perspective. My request for more of God carried a price.

Tears began to soak my pillowcase as He reminded me of my prayers over the previous months, contrasting them with the scenes that had just passed through my mind. I was gripped by the realization that God wanted to make an exchange—an increased manifestation of His presence in exchange for my dignity. After all, I *had* prayed, "at any cost." It's difficult to explain how exactly one knows the purpose for such encounters. All I can say is you *just know.* You know His purpose so clearly that every other reality fades into the shadows as God puts His finger on the one thing that matters to Him.

It was in this place, not knowing if I would ever function as a normal human being again, wondering if I would actually be bedridden for the rest of my life because of this overwhelming presence, that, in the midst of the tears, I came to my point of no return. I gladly yielded, crying, "More, God. More! I must have more of You at any cost! If I lose respectability and get You in the exchange, I'll gladly make that trade. Just give me more of You!"

The power surges didn't stop. They continued throughout the night, with me weeping and praying, "More, Lord, more. Please

> *Face-to-face encounters with God often look very different from each other.... Such experiences have one thing in common—they make it nearly impossible for people to live as they did before they had them.*

give me more of You." Then it all stopped at 6:38 a.m., and I got out of bed completely refreshed. The experience resumed that night and the next, beginning moments after I got into bed.

Later, I learned that what I had experienced was actually a face-to-face encounter with God. If you study such encounters in the Scriptures and in the testimonies of saints, you'll find that face-to-face encounters with God often look very different from each other. He reveals Himself to us according to His purposes, and sometimes He fashions the way He does it according to what He sees in people's hearts. Such experiences have one thing in common—they make it nearly impossible for people to live as they did before they had them.

Trading anything for more of God really is the greatest deal ever offered to mankind. What could I possibly have that would equal His value? I know that many say revival is costly. And it is. But when I get Him in the exchange, I find it difficult to feel noble for what I've paid. Besides, revival only costs in the here and now. The absence of revival will cost throughout eternity.

DIVINE ENCOUNTERS CHANGE US

In 1996 I became the pastor of Bethel Church in Redding, California. I was invited to take that position because the church had been crying out for revival. The church I had been pastoring in Weaverville, California, was experiencing a wonderful outpouring of the Holy Spirit. Bethel was the "mother church" of our church in Weaverville, and because of that connection I was glad to accept their invitation to come and be their senior pastor.

When I first spoke to Bethel's congregation about my coming, I told them that I was born for revival. I said that if they didn't want the move of the Spirit of God—along with the messes that come with such an outpouring[2]—they didn't want me, because revival is not negotiable! They responded positively with close to unanimous support, which was unusual for such a large church.

The outpouring began within a month of our arrival. Lives were changed, bodies were healed, and divine encounters increased in amazing proportions, along with the unusual manifestations that seem to accompany revival. On top of that, approximately one thousand people left the church. This wasn't the kind of revival they wanted. Understandably, it was difficult for people with that opinion to coexist happily with the perspective I held, which was that we should take whatever He gives us until He gives us something else.

Few things are more devastating to pastors than when people leave the church. It often feels like rejection. Pastors are a unique breed—even when people who hate us leave the church, we still feel bad. Yet in this strange season of exodus, my wife and I were immune to the devastation. Usually that is only possible if your heart is calloused to the point where no one can affect you either negatively or positively, or you are in denial about the impact such a loss is causing in your heart. Thankfully, there is one other possibility, and that is that God has actually given you a supernatural grace to live opposite to your circumstances.

Because of the grace given to us, not one day was spent in discouragement or questioning God. Our food really was doing His will. His will provided all the nourishment and strength we needed. Plus, His presence was the reward. The public criticisms and slander, the humiliation of decreased numbers, the daily calls of complaint to our denomination for close to a year—none of it had teeth to its bite. The need for respectability had all but disappeared on the night of my first visitation.

My closest friends could rightly argue that the fear of man was never really strong in my life. And in part that is true. I had learned this from watching my dad in my early years. He displayed the priority of obedience to God regardless of what others might think. Yet God knew what had been lying underneath it all when He asked for my respectability in exchange for the increased manifestation of His presence. It was the kindness of God that made it all possible.

Along with the increased manifestation of His presence, God simply made His will too obvious to miss. God often spoke to my team or me in a dream or a vision. Sometimes He brought forth a prophetic word that confirmed or added understanding to a direction we were to take. There was never a question. The fruit of this move of God was undeniable. It included an increased measure of His presence along with the bounty of transformed lives. That was all we needed to make us smile in the face of such apparent loss. To this day we consider that time of our greatest loss as one of the most precious and delightful seasons of our lives.

THE SIGNS OF HIS FAVOR

When God invades a person's life, things change. Not only that, but the impact of that life on the world also changes. The measure of God's glory that rests upon a life following these unusual divine encounters affects every person we touch. The supernatural becomes natural as God takes center stage in the places where we have influence. When His glory is present, the things that we used to work hard for, such as miracles of healing and transformation in people's personal lives and families, come with little or no effort.

Scripture describes those individuals whose lives are marked by the power and blessing of the living God as those upon whom *God's face shines*. God's countenance is toward His people, and the result is that their lives are marked by His favor. As Proverbs states:

> In the light of a king's face is life, and his favor is like a cloud with the spring rain.
>
> —PROVERBS 16:15

Now is the season when all who confess Christ must give attention to the role of the favor of God in our lives. While He loves us all the same, not everyone has the same measure of favor. I will address this subject of favor in the next chapter.

THE FAVOR
OF HIS FACE

The heart to seek God is birthed in us by God Himself. Like all desires, it is not something that can be legislated or forced, but it grows within us as we "taste and see that the LORD is good" (Psalm 34:8).

For while we have been given the capacity to perceive God's goodness through the new birth in the Spirit, that capacity is something that must develop in us throughout our lives. As Paul explained, "When that which is perfect has come, then that which is in part will be done away.... For now we see in a mirror, dimly, but then face to face" (1 Corinthians 13:10, 12, NKJV).

THE MEASURE OF HIS PRESENCE

The quest for the face of God has two central dimensions—the quest for His presence and the quest for His favor. Let us first consider some of what the Bible has to say about the first dimension: seeking His presence.

First, we must realize that seeking the presence of God is not about trying to get God to do something. He's already given us His Holy Spirit without measure. All measurements are set up on our end of the equation, determined by the degree to which our lives are in agreement with God and His kingdom. Scripture gives us some specific clues about how we can bring our lives into greater agreement with God and "host" greater measures of His presence. Significantly, all of these measures correspond with deeper truths about who God is. If we are going to bring our lives more fully into agreement with God and His kingdom, the primary thing we need is a burning conviction that God is good.

Another foundational revelation about the presence of God is that God actually holds all things together. Colossians 1:17 says, "In Him all things consist" (NKJV). *Consist* means to "hold together." The pantheist worships all things, believing all things to be God. While it is crazy to worship a tree as God, it is correct to realize that God holds every cell of that tree

The quest for the face of God has two central dimensions—the quest for His presence and the quest for His favor.

in place. He is everywhere. And since I can't imagine a place where He isn't, I might as well imagine Him with me. This truth about God brings me into a measure of awareness of His presence.

A more profound truth is that God has come to live in each person who receives Jesus Christ through His work on the cross as the necessary payment for sin. In one sense, He was already in me as the one who actually holds my cells in place. But when I receive Him, He comes to make my body His temple—the eternal dwelling place of God. He has come in an increased measure of His presence.

We progress to a deeper truth when we learn that whenever there are two or three people gathered in His name, He is there in their midst. He is already in me as a part of His creation, and He is in me as His temple, but that measure of His presence increases still more when I come together with other believers in His name. "In Jesus's name" means more than an ending to a prayer. It is in fact the attempt to do and be what He would do and be in that given situation. To gather in His name means that our gathering should look like it did when Jesus met with people two thousand years ago. (If that is a correct definition, then how many of our gatherings are actually *in His name*?)

David discovered a wonderful and even deeper truth that adds to this revelation of increasing degrees of His presence. He said, "You…are enthroned upon the praises of Israel" (Psalm 22:3). His throne is an even greater measure of His presence. He holds my being together with His presence, and then He moves inside to reign as God over my life. He increases my encounter with Him by having me gather with others in Jesus's name. Ultimately, His glory begins to fall on us as we learn the honor of serving Him through thanksgiving, praise, and worship.

This is not a definitive list by any means. But it gives us a place to start in our quest for the greatest treasure of all—God Himself. The point is that the presence of the Lord can and will increase for those who embark on this quest. Isaiah seemed to tap into this understanding when he wrote, "I saw the Lord...with the train of His robe filling the temple" (Isaiah 6:1). The word for "filling" implies that He came into His temple, but He also *kept coming.* That explains why those who seem to have the greatest measure of God's presence on their lives tend to be the hungriest for more. There's always more to hunger for! This shouldn't be a hard concept to embrace, since we believe that He Himself fills the universe with His presence. King David declared that the universe is actually the work of His fingers.[1] That's a really big God who has a lot more to give us than we can imagine.

I cannot live in mediocrity, content with merely knowing that there is more of God to experience and explore—and then do nothing about it. Truths that are not experienced are, in effect, more like theories than truths. Whenever God reveals truth to us He is inviting us into a divine encounter.

His promise "I will be with you always" has to be more than a verse we quote in difficult times. His presence with us is the one factor that could make our impossible assignment to disciple nations a doable command. The promise must become an invitation to discover this increasing manifestation of His presence in our lives so that we might fully enter into our purpose on the earth.

He is to be known through encounters. John 14:16 says, "I will ask the Father, and He will give you another Helper, that He may be with you forever." We will be Spirit filled forever!

Jesus didn't set limits on what we can have in this lifetime. He did set a pace to be followed and not just admired religiously from a distance. Many people are content to live with the *concept* of the presence of God in their lives, but they fail to enter the intended *experience*. When I married my wife, I wasn't interested in the concept or the theory of marriage. I wanted to experience marriage in all its privileges and responsibilities. People who respond to His presence properly can be trusted with increased favor, which we'll look at more in a moment.

We steward the presence of God by learning to obey the commands "Do not grieve the Holy Spirit" (Ephesians 4:30) and "Do not quench the Spirit" (1 Thessalonians 5:19). We grieve Him when we do something wrong; we quench Him when we fail to do what is right, stopping the flow of His love and power that comes from the Father. Jesus modeled what life could be like when a person neither grieves nor quenches the Holy Spirit.

It is for this reason that we see such a great measure of the presence of God in the person of Jesus. John said of Jesus, "I saw the Spirit descending from heaven like a dove, and He remained upon Him" (John 1:32, NKJV). Certainly this is not talking about the indwelling presence of the Holy Spirit that was already in Jesus's life. This was the inauguration of Jesus's ministry, and the Holy Spirit came to rest upon Him as a mantle of power and authority for that specific purpose. But the fact that the Holy Spirit came to rest on Him is evidence of Jesus's faithfulness to be perfectly trustworthy with the presence of God. The same principle is true for us.

The Holy Spirit lives in every believer, but He rests upon very few. Why? It's not because He's fragile; it's because He is holy! Few people give Him a life to rest upon. The one whose life is not in agreement with God—which is what He calls "entering His rest"—has not given Him a place to rest.

In Jesus's Footsteps

Jesus is also our model when it comes to pursuing and increasing in measures of God's favor, as we read in Luke 2:52: "And Jesus increased in wisdom and stature, and in favor with God and men" (NKJV). This is really a remarkable statement. Jesus Christ was perfect in every way, yet even He needed to grow in favor with God and man. It's easier to understand that He needed to grow in favor with man. No doubt favor opened many doors for life and ministry that would have otherwise been closed to Him. But how is it that the Son of God, who was perfect in character and sinless, needed to obtain more favor from God? While I can't answer that question to my own satisfaction, I do know that the implication is quite clear: if Jesus Christ needed to increase in favor with God, I need it much more.

Possibly Jesus obeyed His Father in embracing a life that required Him to grow in favor with God only because of *our* need to learn how to do the same thing. One thing I'm convinced of is that, by Jesus, the Christian life was definitively modeled for every believer. Everything He did in His life and ministry He did as a man who, though He was fully God, had set aside the privileges of His divinity in order to show us a model of the kind of life He would make available to each of us through His death, resurrection, and ascension. For our sakes He showed us how to grow in favor with God.

WHAT IS FAVOR?

In order to grow in favor, you must first have favor. So what exactly is favor? I think we are most familiar with the idea that favor is preferential treatment shown to somebody. It denotes acceptance, approval, and pleasure.

While the Greek and Hebrew words translated "favor" in Scripture include these definitions, there is a deeper dimension to the Greek word for favor: *charis.* Almost everywhere in the New Testament this word is translated "grace." Grace (and favor) is essentially a *gift.* If we gain favor with people or, as we might say, get into their "good graces," we have special access to them and we receive something from them. The same thing is true about gaining favor

God gives us His grace to empower us to become like Christ.

with God, although the *charis* we receive from God is obviously different from the favor we receive from men. At our conversion, we learn that God's grace is His *unmerited favor* toward men through the blood of His Son. This unmerited favor includes not only being forgiven of sin but also receiving access to the very presence of God in the same way that Jesus has access to Him.

Every believer receives this favor from God, but we don't all recognize the additional dimensions to the *charis* we receive. God's grace is also His operational power, the force of His nature. He gives us this grace to empower us to become like Christ.

These two aspects of God's grace—access and power—set us up to understand what it means to grow in favor with God. At the heart of growing in favor are two aspects: (1) the pursuit of God, the practice of coming before God through the "new and living way" (Hebrews 10:20) that Christ has made available to us, and (2) receiving, in God's presence, measures of His own nature that empower us to be conformed into the image of the Son He loves.

Considering the fact that it takes favor to get more favor and that we have all been given a measure of favor with God through our conversion, the issue of growing in favor is an issue of stewardship. The real question is, What have I done with the favor God has given to me?

I believe that the failure to understand and pursue the journey of stewarding the favor of God has led so many people to die in the unnecessary tragedy of never having their God-given dreams and desires fulfilled. Often those same individuals blame others around them for not supporting them in the pursuit of their dreams. The sober reality is that most dreams go unfulfilled because of the lack of favor with God and man. Where favor is increasing, we witness the power of exponential increase that comes through agreement. That is the by-product of favor.

Our authentic dreams from God cannot be accomplished on our own. That is a sure sign that a dream is too small. We must dream so big that without the support that comes through favor with God and man, we could never accomplish what is in our hearts.

While God loves everyone the same, not everyone has the same measure of favor. Yet everyone is positioned to increase in favor *if* each one of us effectively stewards what we have. In other words, when we seek His face from the favor we have, we increase in favor itself.

THE SUPREME ISSUE

As with all gifts, God's favor is given to all of us freely, with no strings attached, and it also comes with a purpose. But not everyone necessarily chooses to use it for its intended purpose, or to use it at all. But God's favor most definitely is something that we're supposed to use.

Jesus taught on the subject when He gave a parable about talents. In His story the word *talent* does not mean a natural ability to do something well. A talent was a sum of money in the ancient world. Because it can be measured, it represents the subject of favor very well, because favor also is a measurable commodity.

> For it is just like a man about to go on a journey, who called his own slaves and entrusted his possessions to them. To one he gave five talents, to another, two, and to another, one, each according to his own ability; and he went on his journey.
>
> —MATTHEW 25:14–15

Just as these servants were each given different amounts of money, not everyone starts out with the same amount of favor. We can't allow ourselves to trip over this—where there is a debate between our idea of what is fair and God's, we'd be wise to stick with God's. God is sovereign (supreme authority, self-governing, not ruled by another), and He decides who starts with what.

"All men are created equal" is not a verse in the Bible. The statement is true as it pertains to God's love, for He loves everyone the same. But not everyone is given the same measure of favor. To consider God unjust because of this is foolish. He is God. And God is love, which means He does everything out of His goodness.

> Immediately the one who had received the five talents went and traded with them, and gained five more talents. In the same manner the one who had received the two talents gained two more. But he who received the one tal-

ent went away, and dug a hole in the ground and hid his
master's money.

—MATTHEW 25:16–18

The servants were given various amounts, "each according
to his own ability." They were given something because they
had the capability to use it. Clearly, proper stewardship is *using*
what we've been given in order to gain increase. Similarly, the
word *traded* here is a word that simply means, "to work with."
The faithful servants put the money to work, just as we must
put the favor we've received from God to work in our lives in
order to bring increase. Now clearly someone who understands
how money works will be able to work with money more successfully than someone who doesn't; in the same way we must seek to
understand the nature and purpose of God's favor if we are going
to put it to work successfully.

God in His wisdom gives us only what we can handle by His
grace as we engage in this learning process. He doesn't expect
us to solve calculus equations before we've learned addition and
subtraction. That's not to say that God doesn't want full maturity in each of us. But He knows that the key to growth at every
stage, whether we're in charge of much or little, is the same. The
primary issue is always faithfulness. God, who is perfectly faithful, is looking for this trait in those who say they love Him.

Now after a long time the master of those slaves came and
settled accounts with them. The one who had received
the five talents came up and brought five more talents,

saying, "Master, you entrusted five talents to me. See, I have gained five more talents." His master said to him, "Well done, good and faithful slave. You were faithful with a few things, I will put you in charge of many things; enter into the joy of your master."

Also the one who had received the two talents came up and said, "Master, you entrusted two talents to me. See, I have gained two more talents." His master said to him, "Well done, good and faithful slave. You were faithful with a few things, I will put you in charge of many things; enter into the joy of your master."

—MATTHEW 25:19–23

Each one of us is given the opportunity for increase by faithful use of what we've been given. In the kingdom of God, faithfulness is the supreme value and is always rewarded. On the other hand, consider God's verdict on unfaithfulness:

And the one also who had received the one talent came up and said, "Master, I knew you to be a hard man, reaping where you did not sow and gathering where you scattered no seed. And I was afraid, and went away and hid your talent in the ground. See, you have what is yours."

But his master answered and said to him, "You wicked, lazy slave, you knew that I reap where I did not sow and gather where I scattered no seed. Then you ought to have put my money in the bank, and on my arrival I would have received my money back with interest. Therefore

take away the talent from him, and give it to the one who
has the ten talents."

—MATTHEW 25:24–28

In this story, the one who started with the most is the one
who was found the most faithful. His responsibility was greater,
and he was duly rewarded. But the opposite can also be true.
I have observed that some of those who seem to have the greatest
opportunities in life end up being the ones who squander them
the most and therefore fall into the greater judgment. They are
held accountable; they must give an answer for their unfaithfulness. Scripture is clear on this point: "From everyone who has been
given much shall much be required" (Luke 12:48). The landowner
honors the slave who started with the most and who earned the
most by giving him the unused talent of the unfaithful slave. The
first slave had the greater responsibility, *and* he proved to be the
most faithful. Faithfulness is what God is looking for:

> For to everyone who has, more shall be given, and he will
> have an abundance; but from the one who does not have,
> even what he does have shall be taken away. Throw out
> the worthless slave into the outer darkness; in that place
> there will be weeping and gnashing of teeth.
>
> —MATTHEW 25:29–30

In the same measure that faithfulness is rewarded, unfaithfulness is judged. God judges everything that opposes love. How
did the lazy servant oppose love? Consider the master's rebuke to
him. Interestingly, he didn't correct the servant's view of him as

a hard man, but he rebuked him for his wrong response to that view. Instead of being inspired by a holy fear of the master, which would have given him a correct sense of the weight of the trust that had been laid on him, he looked at the task and said, "Too hard." In ignoring his responsibility, he was dishonoring his master by essentially telling him that his expectations were too high.

The faithful servants didn't make excuses. They took what they were given and simply used it. They may also have known their master to be a hard man, but apparently they also thought him trustworthy and desired to please him. In fact, in going out and getting more talents with the ones they were given, they were acting like their master. They were aware that they represented the master in his absence and endeavored to rise to his level of doing business. Their love for him was demonstrated in actions that revealed their deep honor and respect for his authority and their sense that it was a privilege to represent him.

I have been disturbed to see the attitude of the lazy servant operating in so much of the church when it comes to fulfilling our commission to imitate Christ in destroying the works of the devil and performing signs and wonders. The favor that we've been given to be like Christ has this commission included in its purpose. It uniquely positions us as representatives of His kingdom to carry out exploits that bring Him honor and to bring people into their God-given destiny. Jesus's words were, "And as you go, preach, saying, 'The kingdom of heaven is at hand.' Heal the sick, raise the dead, cleanse the lepers, cast out demons. Freely you received, freely give" (Matthew 10:7–8).

Faithful servants don't get hung up over *how* they're going to fulfill the Master's command before they've even tried or even after they've tried a few times and been unsuccessful. They trust the Master. If He said it, then apparently He thinks they're up to the task—if they use the talents He's given them. They see that being given the opportunity to represent Him in all His power and glory is the greatest privilege they could ever receive.

Unfaithful servants look at the commands to do the impossible and question the goodness and wisdom of the Master. Instead of pursuing Him to find a way to fulfill His commands, they put them out of sight and go about their business. Ignoring God while pretending to serve Him is a serious violation of relationship and cuts us off from being able to do the very thing we were put on the planet for—to live our lives to honor the One to whom we will give account.

Jesus modeled perfect faithfulness for us by taking on the form of a servant and perfectly fulfilling His Father's will. He showed us that the best service comes from those who aren't actually hired servants, but by intimate friends who take on a servant role as an expression of love.

We have been given favor because it empowers us to serve more effectively. Favor is not to be used to draw attention or people to ourselves. His is a selfless kingdom. When people use the favor of God for personal gain, and not for kingdom purposes, they have chosen where they will level off in their development and experience.

AS IT WAS IN THE BEGINNING

As Jesus showed us, the way to becoming a faithful servant of God is by learning to be His friend. In fact, friendship is the purpose of our creation. Everything in creation was made for His delight and pleasure, but human beings alone were made with the capacity to draw close to God in intimacy. No other part of creation has been given the opportunity of becoming a friend of God, even becoming one with Him through His indwelling Spirit.

In the beginning God walked with Adam in the cool of the garden. His desire to spend time with those who love Him by choice set the stage for all the conquests that were to come. While Adam and Eve were placed in a garden of perfect peace, the garden itself was placed in the midst of turmoil. It was in this original setting that Adam and Eve were given the assignment to subdue the earth. God said, "Be fruitful and multiply, and fill the earth, and subdue it" (Genesis 1:28). As they increased in number they would be able to establish and extend the rule of God over the planet by representing Him as His delegated authorities.

He has chosen us for this purpose, not because we're better, but because we're the ones who signed up. He enlists everyone who is available.

The reason that the territory beyond the garden was in turmoil was that Satan, one of the three archangels, had set up his rule there after being cast out of heaven for his rebellion and his desire to be worshiped like God. God in His sovereignty allowed the devil to set up his rule on planet Earth because His intention was to bring eternal judgment to the devil through mankind, in particular, through the fruitfulness of intimate co-laboring between God and man.

We must always remember that Satan has never been a threat to God. Instead, God chose to give those who were made in His image the privilege of executing the judgment of God on all the fallen hosts. God determined that it would it be fitting for the devil's defeat to come at the hands of those made in the image of God, who worship Him by choice, because it would mean that the devil would be overcome by those who succeeded where he had failed. This divine justice strikes at the very heart of how and why Satan was removed from heaven in the first place.

We see God's divine plan expressed by David in Psalm 23:5—"You prepare a table before me *in the presence of my enemies*" (emphasis added). It's as though God said, "Satan! My people love Me, and I love them, and you're going to watch!" Such romance strikes terror in the heart of the devil and his hosts. At this table of fellowship our relationship with God deepens and overflows into a life of victory in conflict with the powers of darkness.

God is looking for partnership, a partnership in which He empowers His people to become all that He intended them to be. He is the One who said that He made the heavens for Himself, but the earth He made for man. Through this partnership, He portrays the intended similarity between His world (heaven) and ours (Earth). His people are to demonstrate His rule to a dying world.

He has chosen us for this purpose, not because we're better, but because we're the ones who signed up. He enlists everyone who is *available*.

JESUS CHRIST: THE PERSON OF WISDOM

To want to grow in favor with God is the most natural desire in the world. Wisdom knows how.

Wisdom gives us the keys to understand and use the favor that we've been given in accordance with God's purposes in giving it to us. Increase in wisdom and increase in favor go hand in hand for us, because they are interdependent. Jesus, once again, modeled this for us, as we saw in Luke 2:52. He "increased in wisdom and stature, and in favor with God and men" (NKJV). In fact, Jesus is the person of wisdom, as 1 Corinthians 1:30 states: "Christ Jesus...became for us wisdom from God" (NKJV). This should convince us that studying the life of Christ and deepening our relationship with Him are central to stewarding our favor with God.

We should also study Proverbs, the book of the Bible that best expresses wisdom. As such, this book gives us some of the greatest instruction for growing in favor. The following verses from Proverbs give practical instruction for how to pursue an increase of favor.

"Do not let kindness and truth leave you.... So you will find favor and good repute in the sight of God and man" (Proverbs 3:3–4). This statement describes those who embrace the instruction of the Lord with diligence, committed to obey and not to lose sight of His Word. By doing so they position themselves for an increase of divine favor. Placing high value in the voice and Word of the Lord plays a big role in obtaining more favor from God.

"For he who finds me finds life and obtains favor from the LORD" (Proverbs 8:35). The entire eighth chapter of Proverbs reveals the person called Wisdom, which, of course, is Jesus Christ. The chapter primarily focuses on the role of Wisdom in the story of Creation, and in doing so unveils the true nature of wisdom—it is the creative expression of God. This verse promises that finding the wisdom of God as it pertains to His creative expression in our fields of influence is a sure way to increase in God's favor.

One helpful way to see how this promise works is to look at it within the picture we're given in the New Testament, where we are told that we are the body of Christ. Like the members of a human body, every part of the body of Christ is unique, yet each finds its significance and function only in relationship to the rest of the body, particularly the brain. Finding wisdom is the process of discovering and correctly aligning our lives in relationship with the head, Christ, and with our unique destiny to express an aspect of His nature in a way that no one else can. God's favor rests upon us when we are being and doing that which He created us in His wisdom to be and to do.

"He who diligently seeks good seeks favor" (Proverbs 11:27). The word *good* here means "things that are of benefit" or "pleasing." Those who put extra effort in pursuing the things that please the Lord and bring benefit to the King and His people cannot help but increase in favor with God and man.

"A good man will obtain favor from the LORD, but He will condemn a man who devises evil" (Proverbs 12:2). The word *good* here carries several other characteristics that I did not mention in the previous verse. "Pleasant," "cheerful," "gracious," "generous," and "festive" are a few of the definitions that apply to this verse. The world wants to paint "good" people as boring, legalistic, and somber. But God's goodness can always be recognized in those who seem to overflow with joy, encouragement, forgiveness, peace, and generosity. Their goodness is the fruit of a life lived in celebration of their life with God, and because they are like Him, He is drawn to them. Good people are easy to promote. They automatically align themselves for the lifestyle of increased favor.

"Good understanding produces favor, but the way of the treacherous is hard" (Proverbs 13:15). One of the primary commands in the Book of Proverbs is to seek understanding. Many Christians, recognizing that God is opposed to a purely intellectual gospel that is devoid of the Spirit of God and that consists of form without power, have fallen into the error of believing that God values mindless Christianity. But the truth is that none of us will reach maturity if we think we have to dumb down or cut off part of ourselves in order to serve God. If we are going to be successful in fulfilling the assignments that God has for us, we will need all of our faculties and energies to be focused and engaged in what we're doing and what God is doing. After all, we're called to be *disciples*, that is, learners. Jesus certainly sought to bring His disciples into a deeper understanding of kingdom reality. Those who pursue understanding life from God's perspective please Him greatly. Practicing the principles of the kingdom positions a person for an increase in the favor of God.

"The king's favor is toward a servant who acts wisely, but his anger is toward him who acts shamefully" (Proverbs 14:35). To "act wisely" is to live as Jesus would live, with a deep-seated awareness of the King's thoughts and values. Such a lifestyle attracts the King's scepter of favor.

"He who finds a wife finds a good thing and obtains favor from the LORD" (Proverbs 18:22). The implications of this promise go far beyond simply getting married. Many have done that without any increase of God's favor. This promise is given to those who correctly steward the blessing of marriage. If you want to catch the attention of the king, treat his daughter well. By nature, it implies unity—becoming one—which illustrates the relationship of God with His people. The groom is to love his bride as Jesus loves the church and died for her. The bride is to honor and respect the groom as the church respects God. Stewarding marriage by maintaining honor and love in the relationship is to position oneself for increase of favor with God and man. It is when this relationship is held in proper esteem that the message of God's love is most clearly seen in this world.

As you can see from these verses, those who grow in favor are not those who are focused on jumping through hoops and crossing things off the list in order to get God's attention. That's the mentality of a hired servant, not a friend. A friend grows in favor by embracing a life of obedience, motivated by passion for Him and Him alone. This truth is an important factor to remember when pursuing God's favor. Many people want more money, or open doors for their business or ministry, or even greater opportunities for their families. But God's favor is first and foremost about giving us the privilege of knowing Him, simply for the purpose of knowing Him. It could be said that divine favor comes to those who have chosen to keep the main thing the main thing—knowing and loving God. "Let him who boasts boast of this, that he understands and knows Me" (Jeremiah 9:24). Those who are angry with God in their hearts will often look at a subject like this and accuse God of showing partiality, not realizing that divine favor comes to those who have honestly dealt with the issues of the heart.

GOD'S FAVOR AFFIRMS OUR IDENTITY

As I mentioned earlier, we gain favor with God as we pursue His wisdom in order to discover and fulfill the destiny for which He created us. Vital to this process is one of the primary expressions of God's favor—declarations in which He recognizes our identity and asserts His approval and acceptance over our lives. Scripture is filled with these declarations, but there must be moments in the life of every believer in which we hear the voice of our Father speak them directly to us. That's when they become *ours*.

It shouldn't surprise us that we need God to show His favor toward us in this way, because this kind of need for affirmation and approval is wired into our DNA. The pursuit of favor is a normal and deeply rooted human behavior. Everyone has a deep-seated awareness of incompleteness apart from outside recognition and affirmation. Even though the pursuit of man's approval has caused many to fall into an unhealthy fear of man, the basic desire for affirmation is authentic and necessary. When we receive this kind of favor, it increases the effect of who we are and what we've been given to do in life because it taps into the principle of *exponential increase through agreement*. It affirms the fact that *two are better than one* if they are united. With favor our potential increases as the strength of others is added to our own.

At a very early age children can be seen pursuing recognition from someone important to them. "Daddy, watch me! Daddy, watch me!" was heard frequently in my home when my children were about to try something new or courageous. The attention they got from me, and the subsequent cheers of support, were essential building blocks of their self-esteem and confidence in life. While I worked hard to give them my undivided attention in those moments, there was an unusually greater positive effect whenever I spoke highly of them to my friends in their presence. It seemed to communicate to them my *ultimate* sign of approval. That is something I still do even though they are adults now.

SEEKING GLORY FROM GOD

The heavenly Father spoke of His Son, Jesus, in the hearing of bystanders, "This is My beloved Son, in whom I am well-pleased" (Matthew 3:17). The mark of divine favor upon a life is always such a heavenly cry!

The challenge for every one of us is to renew our minds and hearts so that our affections are anchored, keeping God's approval as our supreme goal and reward. If we fail to place our value for the favor of man in its appropriate subordinate position in our hearts, we will be vulnerable to tragedy.

Most of us, in fact, need to break our agreement with the spirit of the fear of man first in order to be free to develop the proper priorities when it comes to God's favor and man's favor. Many people don't recognize that their agreement with that spirit is still operating in their thinking, so they will not venture out in their passion for God without the approval of others. Seeking the recognition of man at the expense of approval from God is foolish at best and completely self-destructive at worst, but it is also the way of this world, and so we must be proactive in dismantling such thinking in ourselves and courageous in resisting the peer pressure to cooperate with it. This is where one of Jesus's warnings comes into play. He warned His disciples of the potential influence, like leaven, on their minds by the religious system

(Pharisees) and the political system (Herod).[2] Both have the fear of man as their common denominator.

Jesus also said, "How can you believe, when you receive glory from one another and you do not seek the glory that is from the one and only God?" (John 5:44) This verse does not teach that honoring people is wrong. That would bring us into conflict with the rest of Scripture. What it does say is that faith cannot coexist with the fear of man, that is, with being more concerned what someone else will think of us for a particular decision than what God thinks of us. This is important for us to note, because it is impossible to please God apart from faith. And the pursuit of favor has everything in the world to do with pleasing God.

Nothing compares with the satisfaction of pleasing the heart of our heavenly Father. Embracing the ultimate quest for His face means becoming a person whose every thought and action is driven by the goal of hearing the declaration from heaven: "Well done!" Thankfully, Scripture is filled with clues as to how to become—and how not to become—such a person. In the next chapter we'll take a look at how the history of Israel gives us rich revelation that defines the kind of relationship God has called us into and the choices we all have to make in walking out that relationship.

CHAPTER 3

HEADING TO THE PROMISED LAND

Jacob is the first person mentioned in the Bible who had a revelation encounter with the face of God. Following his wrestling match with the angel of the Lord, "Jacob called the name of the place Peniel [saying]: 'For I have seen God face to face, and my life is preserved'" (Genesis 32:30, NKJV). Significantly, it was this encounter in which Jacob's name was changed to Israel. Hundreds of years later, God designated the following blessing to be spoken over the nation of Israel:

And the LORD spoke to Moses, saying: "Speak to Aaron and his sons, saying, 'This is the way you shall bless the children of Israel. Say to them: "The LORD bless you and keep you; the LORD *make His face shine upon you,* and be gracious to you; the LORD *lift up His countenance upon you,* and give you peace." So they shall put My name on the children of Israel, and I will bless them.'"

—NUMBERS 6:22–27, NKJV, EMPHASIS ADDED

God wanted the same mark that came upon Israel (Jacob) in his wrestling encounter to be upon Israel's descendants. The people of His name were to be recognized by the blessing of favor and peace in their lives—which comes from His face.

The blessing that He assigned to Israel was the declaration of the favor of His face. Thus, it is through Israel that the rest of humanity has been invited into the ultimate quest.

And it is no mistake that Moses was the one God spoke to about His face shining on His people, because Moses is the second, and certainly more significant, person associated with the revelation of the face of God. Exodus 33:11 tells us that "The LORD spoke to Moses face to face, as a man speaks to his friend" (NKJV), and in Exodus 34 we read that when Moses left these encounters, his own face was shining, reflecting the glory he had beheld. Until Jesus Christ Himself, no other person in Scripture is recorded as being one upon whom the real, physical glory of the

Lord was visible in this way. Clearly Moses had a revelation of the face of God, and we need to turn our attention to what it means.

In order to understand the full significance of who Moses was and the revelation he carried, however, we need first to have a sense of where he stood in the narrative that God had been unfolding in the history of the earth. From the moment that Adam and Eve broke their fellowship with God through sin, God began to carry out His plan to bring mankind back into a relationship with Himself. But throughout the early history of mankind there was a wholesale rejection of God and His ways.

So He chose a man, Abraham, from whom to build a nation, Israel, through which He could illustrate what He always had in mind for the whole of humanity. It was never intended that the people of Israel would enjoy God's love exclusively, but instead that they would become the example of what He offers to everyone.

As we've just seen, the blessing that He assigned to Israel was the declaration of the favor of His face. Thus, it is through Israel that the rest of humanity has been invited into the ultimate quest. When we go deeper, we find that the history of Israel calls us to this quest by revealing the fact that God Himself is on a quest— the quest for our faces, as it were. He is on a quest to restore the face-to-face intimacy with His children that was lost through sin. Perceiving God's pursuit of us through Scripture is a vital ingredient in helping us come to the place where we can under-stand and become possessed by the impulse to pursue Him in the same way He has pursued us—with complete abandonment. Those who embrace the ultimate quest are simply those who have correctly perceived and responded to His invitation for restored relationship.

Perceiving God's invitation to us through the Scriptures, particularly in the history of Israel, is not something that everyone does automatically. In fact, much of the history of Israel is the story of a people who fundamentally *didn't get* what God was inviting them into. Thus, we learn both positive and negative lessons from Israel's history—both how to respond to God and how *not* to respond to Him. As we'll see shortly, this is precisely where Moses stands out—he was one in a million who got it.

But the reason we don't automatically get it is that we have to receive divine grace from God in order to see things from His perspective. This process of perceiving and coming into agreement with God's perspective is called *repentance*. Most of us usually associate this word with being sorry for our sin, and this is appropriate. Scripture tells us that godly sorrow leads to repentance.[1] But being sorry is not repenting. We repent when our sorrow over sin leads us to the place where we receive power from God to change the *way* we think. We may all be able to change *what* we think about, but only God can give us a new perspective on reality. In particular, only God can build a paradigm in our thinking in which we live for and from a relationship with Him instead of going through religious motions and being content simply to know about Him.

This is why Jesus began His ministry with the declaration, "Repent, for the kingdom of heaven is at hand" (Matthew 3:2). Christ came to Earth as the culmination and explicit revelation of God's pursuit of mankind. But without receiving the gift of repentance, the very people He preached to, healed, and died for remained blind to this revelation. *Through His very declaration* He made the gift of repentance available to all who would listen. This is the nature of all of God's commands. He spoke the universe into existence, and when He speaks to us, grace is released in the same way to enable us to accomplish what He has said. Our job is to appropriate that grace through trusting what He has said and stepping out in radical obedience to it.

A History of Favor

Appropriately, the history of Israel begins, just as the Christian life does, with such an act of radical obedience—a man left the human boundaries that had hitherto defined his life and stepped into a journey of total dependence on God's perspective and commands. It was Abraham's response to God's invitation for relationship that qualified him to receive the tremendous favor by which God made a father of no one into the father of a nation. Let's spend some time looking at how the favor of God shaped the history of Israel into a story of redemption that prophesies the ultimate redemption that Christ would accomplish for us.

First of all, I want to clarify that while Abraham's faith enabled him to receive the favor God was offering to him, the story is clear that he was not receiving that offer because of some particular merit or strength he possessed. In fact, from Abraham right on through his descendants, the story tells us that it was God's choice alone that distinguished Israel as a people and that they were chosen because of their *insignificance*. This divine strategy of God, to take the lowly and despised things and use them to display His glory, has been played out over and over again throughout history. The reality is that people are more likely to recognize the mercy of God and give Him glory when He does this. Christ declared this to the apostle Paul when He said, "My grace is sufficient for you, for My strength is made perfect in weakness" (2 Corinthians 12:9, NKJV). And Jesus's disciples experienced this in the religious leaders' response to their preaching: "Now as they observed the confidence of Peter and John and understood that they were uneducated and untrained men, they were amazed, and began to recognize them as having been with Jesus" (Acts 4:13). This reality is one of the primary themes in Israel's history, and it prefigures the life of every believer.

There are two things to notice about the favor that God gave to Abraham. I've mentioned the first thing, which is that this favor had a place to land in Abraham's life because of his faith, which he demonstrated through radical obedience. Radical obedience always gives priority to what God has said over what He hasn't said. When God told Abraham to leave his country of origin, He didn't bother to tell him where he was going. He only made it clear that if he was going to be able to fulfill the assignment God was offering him, he couldn't stay in his old environment. When God only gives us the guidance we need for the moment, it tends to keep us closer to Him. This helps us to learn the all-important lesson of dependence on God—a lesson that every single person marked by the favor of God has to learn. Abraham's willingness to follow God on those terms was what was necessary for God to trust him with his amazing assignment.

The second thing to notice about God's favor was that it was given with a specific purpose in mind. Favor always goes with an assignment. In Abraham's case, that assignment was to build a nation, which meant that the impact of the favor on Abraham's life and every one of his descendants had a momentum and purpose that extended beyond them for generations—in fact, to all the generations that would be a part of the revelation God intended to release on the earth through that nation. Thus, virtually all of the encounters Abraham had with the Lord addressed the generations that God's favor was designed to shape.

In one of these encounters, the Lord said to Abraham, "Know certainly that your descendants will be strangers in a land that is not theirs, and will serve them, and they will afflict them four hundred years. And also the nation whom they serve I will judge; afterward they shall come out with great possessions" (Genesis 15:13–14, NKJV). Though a prophesied captivity may not strike most of us as a sign of God's favor, once again this was simply God's divine setup for displaying His power and perfecting His strength in weakness. And when we come to the particular events by which God's prophecy to Abraham was fulfilled, we discover two extraordinary individuals marked by God's favor—one (Joseph) marked to lead Israel into Egypt, and the other (Moses) to lead them out of it. Like Abraham, both of these men went through testing that prepared them to carry God's favor on their lives and to fulfill their assignments.

After Joseph received the revelation of God's favor on his life through two prophetic dreams, his journey immediately led him into circumstances that seemed to contradict that revelation completely. As he ended up thrown in a pit, sold into slavery, and tossed into prison, I'm sure he had no idea that the Lord's favor on his life was positioning him there to fulfill God's prophetic word over his family. But that, more than any plan of the enemy, was the ultimate truth of his circumstances. Divine favor causes you to rise to the top in your sphere of influence, and the reality is that favor can be recognized more easily if you start at the bottom. Thus, Joseph's darkest hour revealed the extraordinary measure of God's favor on his life. Some would say that ending up in prison proved that he had little favor, but that was not so. The reality was that the favor upon his life was the thing that enabled him to turn his adverse circumstances into the very training process he needed to fulfill the assignment for which that favor had been given.

Amazingly, the favor on Joseph's life was not merely to save his family but also to save the entire nation of Egypt. After all, if God's people were going to be coming out of this nation "with great possessions" in a few hundred years, it needed to be a prosperous nation, not one destroyed by famine. In this way the favor on Israel became very visible to the nation of Egypt. But after Joseph's death God allowed a pharaoh to rise up who perceived the blessed children of Israel with eyes of fear and jealousy, just as He had allowed the enemy, who hated and feared Adam and Eve because of their intimacy with God, to infiltrate the Garden of Eden. This pharaoh, in fact, is one of the clearest representations of the enemy in Scripture, and his reign of oppression over Israel is emblematic of the slavery of the human race to the enemy's kingdom of sin and death.

This brings up another undeniable effect of God's favor—it has a way of provoking those who don't have it. It's a reality that began in the garden and continued through Cain and Abel, Satan and Job, Jacob and Esau, David and Saul, up to Christ and the Pharisees and through every generation of church history. Each scenario simply reenacts the hatred of the enemy for the objects of God's affection. But we can't let this deter us from pursuing the place of favor that God has made available to us. As we've seen, it is when we pursue the glory and intimacy that we were created for that God ends up with the perfect conditions in which to rise up and judge His enemies.

Just as He had prophesied to Abraham hundreds of years before, God had a judgment day planned for Egypt—a judgment earned by their wrong response to a people marked by His favor. And just as He would ultimately do for the human race in the person of Christ, God carried out this judgment by raising up a deliverer for His people.

The story tells us that the favor on Moses's life was visible even when he was an infant. Like Christ, Moses was born into a hostile environment for baby boys. In his fear that a deliverer would rise up, Pharaoh had ordered that all newborn male Israelites be killed. But Moses's mother saw that he was special and protected him as long as she could. Then he came under the protection of Pharaoh's daughter and, remarkably, ended up growing up in Pharaoh's household. When he learned that he was an Israelite, his passion grew to see his own people set free from the cruelty of slavery. He tried to accomplish his destiny under his own power and entered a season of exile that lasted forty years. But this, like Joseph's years in prison, became God's training ground for him, culminating in his stunning commission at the burning bush.

The favor on Moses's life was different from Abraham's or Joseph's because the assignment, to deliver the nation of Israel, required Moses to confront the spiritual principality that was oppressing Israel. Thus, while Abraham, Isaac, Jacob, and Joseph all have stories of God's miraculous power associated with them, the miracles that He performed through Moses are on a completely different scale. It makes it easier to understand Moses's insecurity at the burning bush when we consider that nothing like what God was asking him to do had ever been done before. He was familiar with power. After growing up in Egypt, he probably knew exactly what he was up against when God told him to confront the demonic power behind Pharaoh's throne. But he hadn't yet seen the superior power of God on display. This was where Moses had to step out in radical obedience. In doing so, Moses received a revelation of the God who invades the impossible like no one before or around him. And I believe this level of revelation explains why Moses had such a profound, unique relationship with God.

THE BATTLE FOR WORSHIP

Before we consider Moses's relationship with God in more detail, however, we still need to look at some of the elements of the Exodus story and see how they speak prophetically of our own exodus from the kingdom of darkness into the kingdom of light.

First of all, we can't miss the fact that God invoked His rightful ownership of His people to Pharaoh by demanding that they be free to worship Him. This issue of worship is the defining issue of human history. We were made to worship the One in whose image we were created. Christ was crucified to restore our place of communion with God in worship. That is, the salvation He purchased for us is not only salvation *from* death but also, and even more importantly, salvation *unto* a life of communion with God. In that place of beholding the Lord in worship, we are transformed. Since we always become like whatever we worship, there is nothing greater that God could want for His people than for them to worship Him, for there is nothing greater than Himself. God doesn't long for our worship because He is an egotist in need of our affirmation. Instead He longs for our transformation that takes place in the glory of His presence, the glory that descends in times of extended worship.

When Adam and Eve sinned, they didn't stop worshiping; they simply started directing their worship toward the wrong thing. The enemy's agenda has always been to rob our destinies by getting us to worship anything but God. We see this agenda demonstrated in the Exodus story through Pharaoh, who clearly understood the fact that Israel's worship of God was a threat to his kingdom. His responses to Moses reveal the tactics that the devil still uses today as he tries to keep people from entering into complete freedom, which is the true fruit of our lives when we live to worship the One worthy of our worship. And God's responses to Pharaoh reveal His passion to bring His people into nothing less than complete freedom. Total freedom is always on God's agenda. His love always works to make us free. The anger of God is always aimed at that which interferes with love.

Let's consider the strategies behind Pharaoh's responses to Moses. When Moses first asked Pharaoh to release God's people to go and worship, Pharaoh said, "Go, sacrifice to your God in the land" (Exodus 8:25, NKJV). The devil doesn't mind our worshiping God if it doesn't require change. True worship, and the freedom it brings, requires the dedication of our entire lives to God. Any offer that tries to convince us otherwise is a false one. If we try to keep worship "in the land" of the devil's domain, we give him legal access to influence and spoil our efforts.

When Moses rejected these terms, Pharaoh offered to let Israel go but said, "Only you shall not go very far away" (Exodus 8:28). To allow for changes, but only partial ones, is still an effort to control God's people. This strategy usually works well with those who know it's right to worship God but who are still holding on to something. Such people can often be convinced that fully surrendering their lives to God in worship is too extreme. Consider what happened to the woman who prepared Jesus for His burial by pouring costly ointment over Him—ointment worth a whole year's income. Everyone but Jesus thought it to be excessive and extreme. But Jesus honored her by stating that the story of her extravagant worship would be told wherever His story was told. What others thought to be excessive and extreme, God considered reasonable. The only true worship is extreme worship, and only extreme worship brings extreme results—transformation.

Rejected again, Pharaoh enlarged his offer by saying, "Go now, you who are men" (Exodus 10:11, NKJV). It becomes quite clear that the enemy fears entire families worshiping God together, united in purpose. There is a powerful spiritual agreement that is established when multiple generations join their efforts to honor the one true God, and it brings an exponential release of power and blessing that can't be obtained any other way. The devil knows it, too, and for this reason he seems to work overtime to destroy families. God Himself explains why He made the husband and wife into one—it was so He could have godly offspring.[2] Unity breeds unity, especially when its purpose is to honor God.

Pharaoh's final effort to bring Moses and Israel into compromise is found in his statement, "Go, serve the LORD; only let your flocks and your herds be kept back" (Exodus 10:24, NKJV). This statement reveals the ultimate test and potentially the ultimate place of blessing from God. It is to worship God with all of our financial resources as well as with our families. A Christianity that costs little is worth little. Satan knows that if he can keep us attached to his fear-oriented economy, he can still influence our emotions and will and poison our thinking. The end result is that we become ineffective in reaching our divine purpose. Such a last-ditch effort on the part of Pharaoh reveals what Satan fears most—families who worship together with reckless abandon, using all their assets for the glory of God. This absolutely terrifies the devil, because nothing will be withheld from this kind of people.

And this was precisely the sort of group of people that God intended Israel to be. He didn't send Moses to make a bargain with Pharaoh. All of his negotiations with Pharaoh were set up to earn Israel's trust by displaying God's superior power and to accomplish a deliverance that would prophesy the ultimate deliverance He would bring to the human race through the Atonement. In order to fulfill the latter purpose, the confrontation by which Pharaoh finally capitulated to God's demands was a confrontation in which death came to all those who failed to sacrifice a Passover lamb and anoint their doorposts with its blood. (One of the wonderful truths of this story is that only one lamb was sacrificed per household. I believe that this signifies that there is a covenantal blessing made available to entire families when members of that family walk faithfully before God.)

So, just as the Christian life begins by embracing the grace and forgiveness Christ has provided for us by faith, Israel's deliverance began with embracing that which God had prescribed to them for their protection. The Scripture is clear that if they had failed to trust and obey His instructions, they would have been no more immune to the angel of death than the Egyptians. Their faith was an essential ingredient in their deliverance.

But almost immediately after they took this first step of faith, they found themselves faced with another test. They found themselves between the Red Sea and the Egyptian army. Most of us face this kind of test early in our faith. It seems that God is leading us down a road into a life of impossibly high standards, and we are dogged by the pressure to go back both to sin and to the world. But in Israel's case, the presence of the Egyptian army and the prospect of returning to slavery gave Israel the incentive to cross the sea that had previously looked like an insurmountable obstacle. Had Pharaoh and his army not been on their backside, I doubt very much that they would have had the courage to cross. God is so good that He will even use the enemy to motivate us to get to where we need to be. The devil is a pawn in the hands of the Master—his greatest attempts to destroy are *always* reworked to bring glory to God and strength to His people.[3]

ENTERING HIS FULLNESS

Has there ever been another time in human history in which over a million slaves have suddenly gotten up and simply walked out of the nation where they were oppressed? Other than the life, crucifixion, resurrection, and ascension of Jesus Christ, the Exodus is probably the most astounding thing that has ever happened. But from God's perspective the greater reality for His people was not their deliverance but the *purpose* for their deliverance. The same is true of the salvation that Christ gives to us. The significance and nature of this salvation is something that we will be learning about throughout our lifetimes. It never gets old to meditate on the fact that we were once dead in our sins and have been resurrected as a new creation with a living spirit, in which the Spirit of God dwells. But the truth is that life in the kingdom is a greater reality than our entrance into the kingdom.

This truth is portrayed symbolically by the Exodus story. When the Israelites came out of slavery in Egypt, they passed through the Red Sea. This is a picture of water baptism, the prophetic act by which we declare faith in Christ and receive forgiveness for our sin.[4] God didn't merely bring Israel *out* of slavery; He also brought them *into* the Promised Land. And when He brought them into that new territory, they crossed through another body of water, the Jordan River, into the Promised Land. This speaks of the baptism of the Spirit. (Jesus referred to the Holy Spirit as a river, for example, in John 7:38–39.) The first baptism deals with getting us out of the red, so to speak—paying our debt of sin. The second baptism deals with getting us into the black—getting us filled with God so we can walk with Him and more effectively represent Him as His agents of power on the earth. The promised land for the believer is living life in the realm of the kingdom—the King's domain. This is the realm we were saved to live in.

Many Christians repent enough to get forgiven but not enough to see the kingdom.

In actuality, two and a half tribes decided to live on one side of the river while nine and a half tribes crossed over into the

Promised Land. God required them to work together to make sure that people on both sides of the river came into an inheritance. This "river" continues to be a point of division to this day, as a host of wonderful people have chosen to live on the other side of the river of God's intentions. They are not inferior, nor are they powerless. But they have settled for less. There is more across the river.

What the Exodus story shows us is that it is possible for people to be brought out of slavery but stop short of entering into the land of promises. In fact, the entire generation that came out of Egypt failed to fulfill the destiny God had for them; they died in the small peninsula between Egypt and the Promised Land. The simple reason for these aborted destinies was a lack of repentance— a failure to allow God to retrain their thinking from the slavish mentality of Egypt to the mentality of those fit to walk in covenant with Him.

In the same way, many Christians repent enough to get forgiven but not enough to see the kingdom. As I stated earlier, Jesus's first instruction in His ministry was, "Repent, for the kingdom of heaven is at hand." But just as the Israelites did, such believers miss out on all that is available in the authentic Christian life, and they are in danger of settling for a life of religious form.

Religion is the antithesis of the kingdom of God. And the kingdom—the realm of the King's domain—is what every man, woman, and child longs for deep within their hearts. Religion creates appetites it cannot fulfill. By nature it carries a value for form without power, information without experience. It makes outward appearance a priority over the issues of the heart. For this reason religion does not provide an opportunity to actually know God, and it is therefore cruel, powerless, and boring.

We must be a people who are not willing to sacrifice the ideals of the kingdom for artificial substitutes. This present move of God is all about retraining us to lock into His manifest presence and live for nothing else.

KNOWN BY GOD

The fundamental difference between authentic Christianity and religion is the issue of knowing and being known by God versus merely knowing *about* Him. In fact, the only thing more important than knowing God is to be known by Him. Jesus made that clear in Matthew's Gospel when He warned that the Father would say to some, "*I never knew you*; depart from Me" (Matthew 7:23, NKJV, emphasis added).

Knowing about someone is not the same as knowing him or her. As a child I was a great fan of Willie Mays, the Hall of Fame baseball player with the San Francisco Giants. I read everything I could read about him, collected his baseball cards, attended games, and listened to countless broadcasts of the Giants' games on the radio. I could tell you his birth date, give numerous statistics about his accomplishments on the field, and even show you my copy of his autograph. But I didn't know him, and he didn't know me. For that to happen we would have to spend time together, and then he would have to let me into his life, as I would also need to do the same for him. Only if that were to happen could I say, "I know Willie Mays."

While God knows everything about everybody, He does not know everyone. He can give more facts about a person than anyone could ever know of himself. But a relationship takes mutual consent and cooperation. For Him to know me I must open up my heart and give Him access to the secret things of my life. That is why confessing our sins to God is so important. It is the beginning of the relationship. He already knows all—the good, the bad, and the ugly. But when I confess them to Him, I come into agreement with Him about my sin being wrong. But a relationship must be built on more than confession. That just removes the obstacles and makes a relationship possible. In confessing sin I open myself up to Him to make personal relationship a possibility.

Relationships are built on trust, communication, common interests, honesty, and time together. It is no different with knowing God. And it is from that place of knowing God that we find our greatest purpose in life.

Yet being known *by* God is the most important thing in life, and it won't happen without my surrender and response to Him.

A Kingdom of Priests

God invited Israel to know Him on Mount Sinai when He declared in Exodus 19:6: "You shall be to Me a kingdom of priests and a holy nation." God intended the entire nation of Israel to be priests unto the Lord, giving each citizen unique access to His presence in order to fulfill the amazing honor of ministering to God Himself. This was the heart of God for His people—for everyone to have access to Him. He had brought them out of Egypt to practice this kind of worship.

The giving of the Law at Mount Sinai was intended to facilitate the process by which Israel would unlearn the thinking of Egypt and learn how to walk in their new identity as priests to the Lord. In describing what He required of them, God was unveiling His holy and righteous nature, which they would need to emulate in order to walk in relationship with Him. But Israel rejected God's invitation for relationship. We see this in Exodus chapter 20 during an amazing encounter between God, Moses, and Israel:

> All the people perceived the thunder and the lightning flashes and the sound of the trumpet and the mountain smoking; and when the people saw it, they trembled and stood at a distance. Then they said to Moses, "Speak to us yourself and we will listen; but *let not God speak to us, or we will die.*"
> —EXODUS 20:18–19, EMPHASIS ADDED

One of the most important features of being a minister unto the Lord is to have a heart for the voice of God. He speaks to make us clean—to qualify us to be able to draw near to Him.[5] Rejecting His voice is rejecting His face, as it rejects the opportunity for an authentic relationship with Him. The Israelites were afraid they would die if they heard His voice, not realizing that the death they feared was in the absence of His voice. They not only rejected a relational encounter with God; they chose to have a mediator. There can be no authentic relationship with God for people who prefer a mediator over and above personal encounters.

Israel's response expressed their preference for the law instead of grace. The law consists of preset boundaries that don't require a personal relationship with God. Grace, on the other hand, is based on relationship. Perhaps an oversimplification would be to say that under the law everyone is given the same requirements. Under grace some things change according to God's unique plan for each individual. For example, God may say to one person that he or she cannot own a television, yet He allows another to have several of them in his or her home. Grace is that way. It is relationally based. This doesn't mean that there are no absolutes under grace—quite the contrary. It just means that under grace God enables us to obey what He commands.

> *Rejecting His voice is rejecting His face, as it rejects the opportunity for an authentic relationship with Him.*

Interestingly, throughout Scripture Moses is associated with the Law. We read, "The law was given through Moses, but grace and truth came through Jesus Christ" (John 1:17, NKJV). As a prophetic sign that life under the Law was not what God intended for us in the kingdom (the promised land), Moses, the mediator of that first covenant, died in the wilderness with the first generation of Israelites. Yet as an individual Moses was one of the few people in the Old Testament who understood and responded to God's invitation for relationship. We see this in the rest of the encounter in which Israel demanded a mediator. Because Moses was more familiar with the Lord's voice and walked in a greater revelation of who God is, his perception of all the fireworks God set off on the mountain was completely different. He said:

> "Do not fear, for God has come to test you; and that His fear may be before you, so that you may not sin." So the people stood afar off, but Moses drew near the thick darkness where God was.
>
> —EXODUS 20:20–21, NKJV

The word *fear* occurs twice in this statement. Moses was pointing out that there was a wrong fear of God and a right fear. The wrong kind leads us to hide from God, while the right kind leads us to draw near to Him in purity and reverence. The fireworks on the mountain exposed the fact that Moses was the only one who understood and possessed the true fear of the Lord.

Moses's unique intimacy with the Lord can be seen even more clearly in a situation that arose later between him and his siblings. Aaron and Miriam had been very critical of Moses because of the wife he chose to marry. God didn't bother defending Moses's choice. He simply asked them how they could be critical of one of His friends—more specifically, one of His best friends. God described His relationship with Moses in this way:

Suddenly the LORD said to Moses and Aaron and to
Miriam, "You three come out to the tent of meeting." So
the three of them came out. Then the LORD came down
in a pillar of cloud and stood at the doorway of the tent,
and He called Aaron and Miriam. When they had both
come forward, He said, "Hear now My words: If there
is a prophet among you, I, the LORD, shall make Myself
known to him in a vision. I shall speak with him in a
dream. Not so, with My servant Moses, he is faithful in
all My household; *with him I speak mouth to mouth,* even
openly, and not in dark sayings, and *he beholds the form of
the LORD. Why then were you not afraid to speak against
My servant,* against Moses?"
　　　　　　　—NUMBERS 12:4–8, EMPHASIS ADDED

God had a certain way He would speak with His prophets.
Not so with Moses. Moses was called to greatness as a child and
given the favor that spared his life. But he misused that favor
when he killed the Egyptian in his efforts to fulfill his assignment of becoming Israel's deliverer. The favor of God does
not bless self-promotion. After forty years of tending sheep, he
obtained favor when God came to him in a burning bush. When
he turned aside from his agenda and stepped aside at the burning
bush, God spoke.

His story expands rapidly at this point as God's relationship
with him surpasses all the prophets'—God knew Moses face-to-
face. The glory of God's face would actually rest upon Moses's
face until the people finally asked Moses to put a veil over his

nead—the glory scared them. He is the ultimate example of using favor to increase favor. He had earned a place of trust that gave him access to the secret places with God, to see and experience what others could not have access to. He spoke openly to Moses, not in dark or mysterious sayings that needed an interpretation. Not only that, He also let Moses see His form, which was unheard of.

Now, Aaron and Miriam also had great favor with God. They served in important roles in Israel's daily life. But they didn't have the same place of favor as Moses. As we have seen, it is a truism that God loves everyone the same, but not everyone has the same favor. Moses's pursuit of God earned him a place before God's face that is almost without equal in Old Testament history. The story goes on to tell us that their disregard for this fact almost cost them their lives. God takes it personally when we dishonor those who carry His favor.

There are many self-appointed watchdogs in the body of Christ who have some explaining to do before God. Their Web sites, books, and radio shows are filled with slander and criticisms of some of God's closest friends. Now these friends of God may not always have the best doctrine, and their mannerisms may offend many. They may even have areas of their lives that need serious adjustment and change. But they are recognized in heaven as those who will do whatever the Holy Spirit tells them to do. And the signs that are supposed to follow a believer actually follow them. When people have to disregard the signs that follow a person's life in order to feel justified in their criticisms of that person, they have ignorantly stepped into a place of judgment before God. "Do not slander a slave to his master, or he will curse you and you will be found guilty" (Proverbs 30:10).

We must not forsake our heavenly Father's friends:

Do not forsake your own friend or your *father's friend*, and do not go to your brother's house in the day of your calamity; better is a neighbor who is near than a brother far away.

—Proverbs 27:10, emphasis added

Recognizing the favor of God on another believer plays a huge role in preparing us for the increase of God's favor in our own lives. If I see the favor of God on someone, I am responsible to give honor where it's due. And whoever honors the one that God honors is positioned for an increase of favor from God. Specifically, when we honor those who possess a deeper revelation of God and a deeper intimacy with Him, we position ourselves to receive the same revelation—to be guided deeper into a relationship with God ourselves as we walk in the footsteps of those who are ahead of us. If we are going to develop a heart to know God, we must learn to perceive the lives of His closest friends as examples of what God has made available for us and follow their lead directly to Him.

Consider Moses's life as an invitation to a deeper revelation of God—and be even more encouraged, because he lived in a time in which sin had not yet been atoned for. Jesus, the Son of God, had not yet become a man, dying in our place, paying for our redemption. What that basically means is this—Moses experienced this amazing relationship of friendship with God under an inferior covenant. And it is improper to expect superior blessings from an inferior covenant. The invitation remains: "Whosoever will may come."

At the beginning of the chapter, I stated that the human race has been invited into the ultimate quest for the face of God through the story of Israel, those marked by the blessing of His face. Yet among those Israelites who came out of Egypt, only one embraced this quest. Something should provoke us to find out what possessed Moses to enter "the thick darkness where God was." After all, Moses knew better than the Israelites did that their fear of dying in the presence of God was far from unfounded. God explicitly told him, "You cannot see My face, for no man can see Me and live!" (Exodus 33:20). There is no question; to see the Lord in His fullness will kill anyone. We are not wired to be able to withstand that measure of glory, holiness, and power. Yet, apparently Moses felt that knowing more of this God was worth risking death. And later, the same God who had said that any who saw His face would die declared that He spoke to Moses face-to-face. What are we to make of this?

Interestingly, there are several other characters in Scripture who acknowledged that they saw God's face and were stunned to find that they were still alive. I mentioned Jacob at the beginning of the chapter. Gideon and John the Revelator are two more examples:

Now Gideon perceived that He was the Angel of the LORD. So Gideon said, "Alas, O Lord GOD! For I have seen the Angel of the LORD *face to face.*" Then the LORD said to him, "Peace be with you; do not fear, *you shall not die.*"

—JUDGES 6:22–23, NKJV, EMPHASIS ADDED

"I, John…was on the island called Patmos because of the word of God and the testimony of Jesus. I was in the Spirit on the Lord's day, and I heard behind me a loud voice like the sound of a trumpet.…Then I turned to see…*I saw one like a son of man,* clothed in a robe reaching to the feet, and girded across His chest with a golden sash. His head and His hair were white like white wool, like snow; and His eyes were like a flame of fire. His feet were like burnished bronze, when it has been made to glow in a furnace, and His voice was like the sound of many waters. In His right hand He held seven stars, and out of His mouth came a sharp two-edged sword; and *His face was like the sun shining in its strength.* When I saw Him, I fell at His feet like a dead man. And He placed His right hand on me, saying, "*Do not be afraid;* I am the first and the last, and the living One; and I was dead, and behold, I am alive forevermore, and *I have the keys of death* and of Hades."

—REVELATION 1:9–10, 12–18, EMPHASIS ADDED

John didn't die; he only fell "like a dead man." And yet, it was not the same John that left that encounter. He, along with every person who encountered the face of God in Scripture, "died" in

69

ise that the person they were before the encounter and the person they were after the encounter were two different people.

Seeing God is costly. Something in us always dies. But it's only the part that is hindering us from becoming more like Jesus. It's like the sculptor who was once asked what he was going to carve from a particular piece of stone. His response was, "An elephant." Fascinated with his abilities, the observer asked how it was that he could actually carve an elephant out of stone. The artist responded, "Oh, that's easy. I only chip off of the rock the parts that don't look like an elephant." That is exactly what God does to us in our growing experience with Him. He cuts off (brings death to) the parts that don't look like Jesus. And there's no clearer way than through personal encounters with Him.

What seems clear to me is that Moses and those who had personal encounters with God stepped into realms of truth that are simply not accessible to those who are content with the letter of the law and knowledge about God. The Bible can seem like a confusing, even contradictory book because it tells the stories of both kinds of people—those who choose relationship with God and those who choose religion, as well as God's different responses to them both. We see in these examples the stories of those who saw God and didn't die even though the Bible says they would. God intentionally includes these kinds of paradoxes in the Bible because they work to divide those who have a heart to know God from those who simply want to know about God. Jesus taught in parables for the same reason—so that only those who had a heart for Him would come to understand them.

In fact, the entire Bible was written with this assumption: only those who have a personal relationship with God will truly be able to understand it. To those outside of a relationship with God, the things that are only understood in the context of intimacy with God appear to be in conflict. Those who don't realize this live with an arrogant assumption that they have found weaknesses and inconsistencies in the Scriptures. Yet God has used His own willingness to appear weak to expose pride and independence in people. Those who see the pride of their ways have the opportunity to repent. Those who don't see and repent get harder in their hearts until a shaking brings a breaking.

He often chooses to lead us deeper into this knowledge by putting His favor on individuals that we would never have thought of as ideal candidates. It's our job to learn that this is one of His ways. We need to humble ourselves and learn to recognize the favor of God wherever it rests. As a pastor I sometimes invite speakers who come in a rough package but carry a great anointing. I do this to train my congregation to recognize the anointing and to celebrate who people are, not who they aren't. People want to be doctrinally safe, not relationally safe. Often people expect me to publicly rebuke a previous speaker for teaching against what we believe. I will do that only if it's actual heresy. *Heresy* has become the term used to describe anyone who disagrees with a particular leader, but that is not so. We need to give more grace to those who differ from us. The essential doctrines of the church—the Virgin Birth, the divinity and humanity of Jesus, the Atonement, and the like—qualify as issues we should fight for. That being said, I will purposely bring speakers into our church that I know I disagree with theologically *if* they are people of great anointing and integrity. It makes people nervous. But that's not necessarily a bad thing. Insecurity is *wrong security exposed*.

We are coming out of a season where people gathered around doctrinal agreement and formed organizations we call denominations.[6] In recent years the Spirit of the Lord has been bringing about a shift. People are correctly changing their priorities by starting to gather around fathers. In the past the church has often sought for a safety in doctrine at the expense of the profound safety that is only found in godly relationships.

In order to gain a heart that longs to know God, we must sacrifice our need to be right, to understand or explain things. We have to trust Him enough to let Him shatter our boxes of understanding and lead us into deeper realms of His truth. He promises to take us line upon line, precept upon precept[7] and "from glory to glory" (2 Corinthians 3:18). He didn't bring us out of Egypt to camp out in the wilderness, but to take us into the promised land of ever-expanding life in the knowledge of Him.

We also have to recognize that full repentance and transformation can only take place through real encounters with God—through actual experiences with His power and grace. Moses had a divine perspective because he had been exposed to the power of God more than anyone else in Israel. All throughout Scripture, God invites us to experience Him as we read the stories of His encounters with past saints. He invites us to "taste and see" that He is good.

Yet many followers of Jesus Christ are satisfied with the simple promise of going to heaven instead of seeing that their destiny is to press in for encounters with the face of God and live in the corresponding increase of favor. They are satisfied with figurative promises, not their fulfillment. To some people, this may seem like a strength, but it works against the very promises of God, which were given to us for our life on Earth as much as our life in heaven. In fact, God gave us His promises so that as we appropriate them, heaven could come to Earth. I'll say it again: we can only live in the kingdom, our promised land, if we are willing to embrace the adventure of experiencing God as He is.

And so I challenge you to count the cost and, like Moses, to step boldly into the thick darkness where God is. There is nothing worth more on this earth than encountering His manifest presence and responding to the invitation to know and be known by Him. It is what we were made for, what we were saved for, and the only thing that will satisfy the deepest longings of our hearts.

CHAPTER 4

HIS MANIFEST PRESENCE

One of the greatest promises in Scripture is that the Holy Spirit would be poured out upon all of mankind in the last days. This promise is most memorably stated in Joel 2:28: "And it shall come to pass afterward that I will pour out My Spirit on all flesh" (NKJV). We can recognize this promise elsewhere in Scripture by paying attention to biblical prophetic imagery. The primary image associated with the Holy Spirit in the prophetic books of the Old Testament is *water*. We find this metaphor in such verses as Psalm 72:6: "He shall come down like rain upon the grass before mowing, like showers that water the earth" (NKJV). In a similar way, Hosea 6:3 says, "He will come to us like the rain, like the latter and former rain to the earth" (NKJV). And the parallelism is perhaps most clearly seen in Isaiah 44:3: "For I will pour *water* on him who is thirsty, and floods on the dry ground; I will pour My *Spirit* on your descendants, and My blessing on your offspring" (NKJV, emphasis added).

At times the prophets refer to "rivers," "streams," "springs," or "pools," and at other times they use the terms "rain" or "outpouring." But the most interesting part of studying the image of water in the prophetic books of the Bible is the fact that no matter the problem the people of God were having, water seemed to be the answer. In other words, whether they were facing a military conflict, a moral collapse, or even a natural drought, the answer was always the same—they needed the Holy Spirit. The outpouring of the Spirit really is the Bible's cure-all. It's not that there aren't things we are supposed to do in the natural; it's just that in the end we need more of Him than anything else. And He comes like rain—in heavenly downpours!

THE LAST DAYS

On the Day of Pentecost, Peter declared that the promise of Joel 2 was fulfilled.[1] The remarkable events of that morning were all part of an outpouring of the Holy Spirit. Yet, that day was only the initial fulfillment of the promise—the Spirit was poured out on that day, but there is a day coming in which He will truly be poured out on *all flesh*. This is a fulfillment of the promise of the

Spirit being poured as the early and latter rain. The early rain was the first century, and the latter is now.

This ultimate fulfillment of Joel's prophecy will take place as the church enters her finest hour of impact in the world. Tragedy comes when the church skims over the great exploits in history and assumes that our finest hour is in the past. This misreading of history derives from a misunderstanding of God's nature. He always saves the best for last—so much so that Jesus even saved the best wine for the end of the wedding celebration.[2] And when He restores things that are destroyed or broken, He restores them to a place greater than before. For example, Job lost everything in the devil's assault on his life. But when God restored him, he was given twice what he lost. It is God's way. To expect anything less of Him for the last days is at best pure ignorance or at worst unbelief.

> The outpouring of the Spirit really is the Bible's cure-all.

The church is destined by God to fulfill a particular assignment in the last days, and the promised outpouring of the Spirit is directly connected with that assignment. We have been commissioned to do what Jesus did and teach what Jesus taught so that we might be able to fulfill the assignment to disciple nations. The outpouring of the Spirit comes to anoint the church with the same Christ anointing that rested upon Jesus in His ministry so that we might be imitators of Him. Only when Jesus Christ, who is called the Desire of the Nations, actually lives through His people can we be successful in His command to disciple nations.[3]

It is in the heart of God for His people to actually represent (or "re-present") the aspects of His nature that people hunger for. He must be expressed through us. God has set us up to be successful at representing Christ by giving us the promise of His Spirit who would come upon us in power. Peter expressed this wonderfully when he said that we "have been given…exceedingly great and precious promises, that through these [we] may be partakers of the divine nature" (2 Peter 1:4, NKJV).

Before we look at what the outpouring of the Spirit is, I want to clarify how it is different from the indwelling presence of the Spirit in the life of the believer. Scripture teaches us that every believer receives the Spirit as the seal and down payment of our full inheritance, which is God Himself.[4] We are heirs of God and have the wonderful privilege and joy of being His dwelling place. The indwelling presence of the Spirit comes about at our conversion, when the Spirit of resurrection brings our spirits to life, just as He breathed into Adam's nostrils in the garden and he became a living being. In the lives of Christ's disciples, we see this take place in John 20:22, when Jesus met with them, "breathed on them and said to them, 'Receive the Holy Spirit.'" But at His ascension, Jesus told these same people that the Holy Spirit was going to come upon them. The Holy Spirit was already in them, but He was going to come upon them with power in order to make them witnesses.

As the word *outpouring* suggests, this promise is fulfilled as the Spirit of God comes upon His people like rain. In such seasons God permeates all we are and do with deluges of Himself. This heavenly invasion of God into our lives is God's first answer to the prayer Jesus taught us to pray: "Your kingdom come. Your will be done, on earth as it is in heaven" (Matthew 6:10). Paul taught us that "the kingdom of God is…righteousness and peace and joy in the Holy Spirit" (Romans 14:17). That is, the kingdom of God is in the Holy Spirit. When He is poured out on us, the King's domain becomes manifested in our lives. This kingdom first creates heaven on earth in the "earth" of our lives, which enables us to mature as co-laborers with heaven in order to bring transformation to the earth around us. Thus, the outpouring of the Spirit deals directly with God's destiny for humanity. The purpose for which Christ accomplished salvation for mankind was just this, to put us right with God so that He could rest upon us, creating a people who could co-labor with Him to bring heaven on earth.

As we first see in the events of Acts 2, the outpouring of the Spirit is intrinsically linked to the baptism in the Holy Spirit. This experience has been the subject of debate for decades. But there was no debate when it was given to the church two thousand years ago. It was so essential to the believer's life that Jesus warned the disciples not to leave Jerusalem before they received it. What's even more important to notice is that some time after that initial experience, we find the disciples getting another level of that same outpouring in Acts 4:30. If the baptism of the Spirit was promised for the last days, and if it was the key to the disciples' success when they began to obey Christ's command to disciple nations, then it seems clear that it is the key for every believer and every generation in the last of the last days. As the church, we must continue with that assignment until it is fulfilled.

The best ground for us to stand on when considering the baptism of the Spirit is the Scriptures. Much of the confusion and debate that has arisen over this issue derives from people evaluating it on the basis of their experience, or lack of experience, rather than inviting the Holy Spirit to bring their level of experience into alignment with what He has already declared. Those who intentionally ignore elements of Scripture that are outside of their experience betray a lack of trust in the God who wrote it. And because faith is essential to please God and know Him, those who resist such experiences and teach others to do the same rarely have the profound encounters with God and the corresponding miracles taking place in their lives. In fact, those who, because of their fear and unbelief, are satisfied with their lack of experience work the hardest to justify their stance by opposing those who teach and pursue encounters with God. A simple examination of Scriptures and the lives of those who teach and experience the baptism of the Spirit will provide overwhelming evidence that this promise of the Father was given to "you and to your children, and to all who are afar off, as many

> *The kingdom of God is in the Holy Spirit. When He is poured out on us, the King's domain becomes manifested in our lives.*

as the Lord our God will call" (Acts 2:39, NKJV). All who are called to salvation are in line to receive this promise of the baptism in the Holy Spirit.

I was raised with the teaching that speaking in tongues is the initial evidence of the baptism of the Holy Spirit. That's not a point I'm willing to go to war over, though I will go so far as to say that this gift of praying in tongues is available to every believer who receives this baptism. As the apostle Paul said, "Do not forbid to speak in tongues" (1 Corinthians 14:39). I personally feel that the baptism itself and its purpose are infinitely more important than the question of what is or is not the initial evidence of the experience. This profound encounter with God is given to us so that we might be filled with His power and be enabled to authentically demonstrate the life of Jesus before this world.

Unfortunately, many can pray in tongues but have little power in their lives. Their example has hurt those who are looking for evidence that this is still a promise of the Lord that is for us today. Somewhere along the line they have bought into the lie that once they can pray in tongues they have all that was promised. Such a response is akin to Israel crossing the river into the Promised Land, camping on the banks of the Jordan, and never going in to take possession of the actual land that was promised. While the gift of tongues is one I take great delight in every single day of my life, there must be more about the ultimate experience in life than to be given a tool to use for personal edification. That is the purpose for that gift. All the other gifts are to be used so that I might be able to represent Jesus in power to the world and affect the course of world history. Therein lies the purpose for such a baptism—power!

God's ultimate provision for the believer in the outpouring of the Spirit is for us to become "filled with all the fullness of God" (Ephesians 3:19, NKJV). For the apostle Paul, it was so obvious that we were to be filled with the Spirit that he actually commanded it.[5] It is one thing to get accustomed to the idea of God actually wanting to live in us. But it's quite another to realize that God intends to fill us with His fullness. I cannot comprehend such a promise. But I know that His purpose in filling us is so that He can overflow through us to the world around us. A glass of water is not really full until it overflows. Similarly, the fullness of the Spirit in our lives is measured by the overflow of the Spirit through us in order to touch the world around us.

WHY POWER?

It would be incorrect for me to say that everything we experience is for the sake of others. That simply isn't true. Some think that God will heal them so that a relative or friend will get saved. Of course it is a great side benefit of a miracle that others are touched by God's goodness. But it distorts the issue.

God delights in us and showers us with blessings just because we belong to Him. He delights over us and gives us access to realms of God simply for our pleasure. Yet there is also an overriding principle in this kingdom: it is nearly impossible to experience more of God and keep it to ourselves. As stated by Peter and

John: "For we *cannot stop* speaking about what we have seen and heard" (Acts 4:20, emphasis added). This is the nature of a life with God—giving is the most natural thing to do.

The kingdom of God must never be reduced to talk, ideas, and principles. The kingdom of God is power.[6] Unlimited power has been granted to those who encounter Him over and over again. Each encounter works deeper in our hearts, bringing about the needed transformation so that we might be entrusted with more of Him. The more profound the work of the Spirit is within us, the more profound the manifestation of the Spirit flowing through us. That in essence is the purpose behind the promise found in Ephesians 3:20: "Now to Him who is able to do far more abundantly beyond all that we ask or think, *according to the power that works within us*" (emphasis added).

A glass of water is not really full until it overflows. Similarly, the fullness of the Spirit in our lives is measured by the overflow of the Spirit through us in order to touch the world around us.

Notice that what goes on around us is *according* to what goes on inside of us. That qualifier is all too often overlooked. This power enables us to present Jesus to others in a way that meets every human need. This lifestyle thrives on the impossible. Our delight is seeing the impossibilities of life bend their knee to the name of Jesus over and over again. Those who encounter Him on this level are much more prone to take risks so that miracles would happen. The absence of the supernatural is intolerable. When you consider the amazing provision of the Lord for those who surrender all, powerlessness becomes inexcusable.

This purpose was announced by the psalmist: "God be gracious to us and bless us, and *cause His face to shine upon us*—that Your way may be known on the earth, Your *salvation among all nations*" (Psalm 67:1–2, emphasis added). Once again there is a profound connection that must not be ignored between the face of God shining upon His people and the salvation of souls among the nations. There is a connection between the two that must not be ignored. Many resist the blessing of the Lord because they don't want to be selfish. Yet it is His blessing upon His people that is supposed to turn the hearts of the unbeliever to the discovery of the goodness of God.

THE ULTIMATE PROMISE

God made a promise that combined two of the greatest experiences for the believer contained in the whole Bible—the outpouring of the Spirit and the encounter with His face. As we will see, they are in essence one and the same. He put it this way, "I will not hide My face from them any longer, for I will have poured out My Spirit on the house of Israel,' declares the Lord GOD" (Ezekiel 39:29). In this declaration, this extraordinary *promise* has been linked together with fulfillment of the ultimate *quest*.

This is stunning news—God's face is revealed in the outpouring of the Holy Spirit! When the Holy Spirit comes in power to transform lives, churches, and cities, the face of God is within reach. His face expresses the heart of who He is and what He is like.

But not all can recognize God's face in the outpouring of His Spirit. When the rain of the Spirit comes, most people fixate on the effects of the storm and miss the One revealed in the cloud. The extreme joy, the weeping, the shaking and trembling, the visions and dreams, the healing, the deliverance, and the manifestation of the gifts of the Spirit, including tongues and prophecy, all are revelations of His face. Some people love these manifestations, and

> *God's face is revealed in the outpouring of the Holy Spirit.*

some people reject them. But the sobering thing to realize is that our response to the move of the Spirit is not a response to manifestations. Rather, it is a response to the face of God. To reject the move of the Spirit of God is to reject the face of God.

MOSES SAW WHAT OTHERS COULDN'T

The degree to which we perceive the face of God through the manifestations of His presence is largely determined by what is in our hearts. As we explored in the previous chapter, there is a great contrast in the way Moses experienced God and the way the people of Israel experienced Him. Moses's heart to know God gave him access to revelation that the people of Israel never perceived. Moses was allowed to see God's form, and Israel wasn't. Also, Psalm 103:7 states that Moses knew the ways of God, and Israel knew His acts.

The ways of God are discovered through the acts of God, but they are only recognized by those who are hungry for Him. For example, whenever we see an instance of God's provision, that provision is a sign. A sign points to something greater than itself. In this case the sign of provision points to God, the provider. Taking time to recognize where a sign points to is not that complicated. However, our value system, which grows from the affections of our hearts, determines whether we will be motivated to take that time. If our value system places more importance on what God does than who He is—if we are religiously motivated rather than relationally motivated—we will not be drawn to recognize the greater revelation behind God's acts. The sad reality is that some are satisfied with what God can do and have little concern for who God is. Such a preference is costly in the long run. Many have missed out on the purpose for their creation by settling for the acts of God, thus failing to come under the influence of the face of God—the ultimate quest and our ultimate destiny.

We need to pay a price to see more clearly. Moses's whole life groomed him to see God. His success as Israel's leader depended entirely on his ability, moment by moment, to perceive and follow the presence and voice of the Lord. But at one point God gave him the opportunity to be successful as Israel's leader in a different way. He offered to assign an angel to take the people of Israel into the Promised Land. This angel would have made sure that every success came to Moses as God promised.[7] But Moses was hungry for God alone, not merely for what God could do to make him successful. He insisted on following the presence of God Himself, saying, "If Your presence does not go with us, do not lead us up from here" (Exodus 33:15).

Moses was the great leader he was because he was not focused on personal success but on the God who could be known. Moses preferred the wilderness *with God* to the Promised Land *without God*, a noble choice for sure. Many in our ranks have failed that test. They have chosen the gratification of fulfilled dreams over the realms of God that seem so costly. They chose the inferior and lost out on the heavenly realities that were at hand, yet unseen. Heavenly realms are made available to us in this lifetime. They are not reserved just for eternity.

Now Israel was also given multiple opportunities to pursue and encounter the manifest presence of God as Moses did. Their entire life was built around the tabernacle, which was set in the middle of the camp of Israel. The presence of the Lord was manifested before them day and night. Interestingly, God manifested Himself to them according to their surroundings—at night there was the pillar of fire, and in the day there was a cloud. In the passages below we see that God also spoke to them face-to-face. But they did not recognize the day of His appearing:

So watch yourselves carefully, since *you did not see any form* on the day the LORD spoke to you at Horeb from the

midst of the fire, *so that you do not act corruptly and make
a graven image for yourselves* in the form of any figure.
—DEUTERONOMY 4:15–16, EMPHASIS ADDED

The LORD *spoke to you face to face* at the mountain from
the midst of the fire.
—DEUTERONOMY 5:4, EMPHASIS ADDED

These words the LORD spoke to all your assembly at the
mountain *from the midst of the fire, of the cloud* and of
the thick gloom, with a great voice.
—DEUTERONOMY 5:22, EMPHASIS ADDED

He spoke to them face-to-face from the cloud. In other words,
there was a revelation of His face in the cloud. But His unwilling-
ness to allow them to see any form of His likeness was because
they were prone to idolatry and would most likely create an image
to represent His form. Today we fall into the same trap when we
create formulas to represent kingdom revelations. People are often
tempted to look for shortcuts to kingdom benefits, resulting in
Ishmaels instead of Isaacs—counterfeits instead of the real thing.

However, as I mentioned, God did allow Moses to see His
form. God could trust Moses with this level of revelation because
his heart had been tested. In His mercy, God gives us the level of
revelation that our character is prepared to handle. At the same
time, He continues to reveal Himself in order to expose our character and invite us to know Him more. We see this in the following fascinating encounter in John 12:

"Now My soul is troubled, and what shall I say? 'Father, save Me from this hour'? But for this purpose I came to this hour. Father, glorify Your name." Then a voice came from heaven, saying "I have both glorified it and will glorify it again." Therefore the people who stood by and heard it said that it had thundered. Others said, "An angel has spoken to Him." Jesus answered and said, "This voice did not come because of Me, but for your sake."

—JOHN 12:27–30, NKJV

This encounter reveals the primary responses that people have to the manifest presence and voice of God. Some who heard the voice thought it had thundered. In other words, they classed the experience as a natural phenomenon. Others believed that an angel had spoken to Jesus. These people recognized that something spiritual or supernatural was going on, but they believed it wasn't for them. Jesus, on the other hand, heard the voice clearly and knew that it *was* for them. He had the heart of His Father, which made Him capable of perceiving not only His Father's voice but also the purpose behind it—to communicate His heart to His people. The Father spoke to make something known to all who could hear. But in doing so, He exposed the level of perception that all those standing by actually possessed.

ALL CAN PERCEIVE

Through Christ, God has made it possible for every person to see the kingdom. Our conversion experience gives us access to that realm, as Jesus explained to Nicodemus, "Most assuredly, I say to you, unless one is born again, he cannot see the kingdom of God" (John 3:3, NKJV). However, it is our responsibility to develop this capacity, to train our senses to perceive God through renewing our minds and feeding the affections of our hearts on the truth. Otherwise, we will have no internal paradigm to keep us in tune with the truth amid the prevailing cultural attitudes that surround us.

In the Western world this is a challenge, because we live in a culture that has embraced an almost entirely materialistic worldview. This worldview rules out spiritual reality and makes the physical, material realm the definition of reality. When a materialist encounters spiritual things, he has no box in which to put them. He either has to ignore them completely or explain them by natural means, like the bystanders who said God's voice was simply thunder. Unfortunately, this paradigm influences many believers, leaving them crippled in their ability to perceive and understand the truth of Scripture and the spiritual dimensions of their own lives, let alone supernatural encounters with God.

The conflict between a materialistic worldview and a biblical one is apparent in the inability or refusal of some Western doctors to acknowledge that their patients have been healed by a miracle of God. We know of many people who have gone to their doctors after being healed in order to have a test that would show that they are no longer in the same condition. Though these doctors were the ones who best know the condition that the person was in and they have personally administered these tests, we often hear that many of them will insist that the problem is in remission, or hiding, rather than acknowledging that the person has been healed. Their rationale is that because it is impossible for AIDS or hepatitis C to go away, it must be in hiding. In their field, that's what it looks like to be realistic. But that realism ignores a superior reality—that of the kingdom of God. There are people who have had no evidence of a particular disease for many years whose medical records still declare that they have it, simply because the doctor will not, or is unable to, acknowledge that the person has been miraculously healed. Without that element in their thinking they will constantly fight against the acknowledgment of God acting on behalf of mankind. Thankfully there are a growing number of doctors who not only acknowledge miracles but also personally pray for their patients to experience a much-needed miracle.

One of our own doctors from Bethel Church was working with another doctor and several nurses on a patient who was in a medical crisis. When the patient began to manifest a demon, the others didn't know what to do. Our doctor leaned over that person and quietly bound the devil and commanded it to leave. It did, and the person on the stretcher was filled with peace. The others in the room were stunned at the manifestation of a demon and the ease at which the name of Jesus solved such a problem. They now know there is a spirit world, and they know who to call if demons manifest! They also know that there is another influence in people's lives besides the physical body and the soul (mind, will, and emotions).

The sobering thing to realize is that every time we are exposed to the miraculous—to the acts of God—we are responsible. That is, power forces us to respond. And our responses, either of faith or unbelief, shape who we are. Unbelief hardens us to God, while faith makes us more alive to Him, more capable of knowing and perceiving Him.

POSITIONING OURSELVES FOR ENCOUNTERS

Jacob's conclusion to his first encounter with God is remarkable. After wakening from the dream in which he saw a ladder standing between Earth and heaven with angels ascending and descending upon it, he said, "Surely the LORD is in this place, and I did not know it" (Genesis 28:16).

It's possible to be right next to God and not know it! I often see this truth played out in life. It never ceases to amaze me that in the same meeting one person can be experiencing a powerful touch from the Lord, and at the same moment the person next to him is wondering when the meeting will be over so he can go to lunch.

There are two things that we should learn from this fact. The first thing to realize is that it is possible to position ourselves to encounter God by learning to recognize the signs of His presence, not only as we experience them but also as others experience them. My hunting dog is trained to "honor the point" of the other dogs he is hunting with. That means that he "points," even when he has not yet picked up a scent of his prey. He assumes the same posture to give me a signal that he has found something. He takes the same posture that the other dogs have. As a result, he eventually picks up the same scent that they have picked up. Likewise, when we recognize that others around us are connecting with the presence of God, even when we are not yet aware of Him ourselves, we set ourselves up to become aware of Him by acknowledging His presence on the basis of others' experience.

The disciples learned a challenging lesson in Mark 16:14 in this regard. Jesus rebuked them because "they had not believed those who had seen Him after He had risen." Learning to believe God through another person's experience is one of the most difficult, yet important, lessons in life. Because the Holy Spirit lives within us, we are required to recognize when someone is telling us the truth even when we don't understand.

The second thing to realize is that when God does lift the veil of our senses to perceive what is going on in the spiritual realm, we are not spectators who have stumbled upon something that has nothing to do with us. God is communicating with us and allowing us to see what He sees in order to invite us to know Him and partner with what He is doing.

It is a mistake to think that only certain people with unique gifts can hear and see God. If I think that it's only for others, then I will disqualify myself because I know I'm nothing special. In doing so I remove myself from active faith. One of the essential gestures of faith is to live with the expectation that the God who said that His sheep hear His voice and who gave His life to restore relationship with each of us would like to communicate with us. This faith leads us to lean into His voice—to learn as the prophet Samuel did to say, "Speak, Lord, for your servant is listening." Significantly, it was as soon as he learned to take this posture that he gained access to the greater revelation that God had been inviting him into.

HE IS LOOKING FOR THOSE HE CAN TRUST

God has combined the ultimate quest with the promised outpouring of the Spirit because the ones He intends to clothe with the same anointing that rested upon His Son are those who have the same heart for the face of God that Jesus possessed. Only those with His heart can be trusted to use His power for its intended purpose—to represent Him in all His glory and goodness. This is our challenge—and our destiny.

CHAPTER 5

JESUS: THE FACE OF GOD

*N*ow I want us to turn our attention to Jesus, but before

that, let's look at His forerunner, the prophet named John

the Baptist. Jesus said of him, "Truly I say to you, among

those born of women *there has not arisen anyone greater than*

John the Baptist! Yet the one who is least in the kingdom of

heaven is greater than he" (Matthew 11:11, emphasis added).

Others in Scripture had more dramatic experiences with

God. Others did greater exploits against disease, storms, and

death itself. Some called down fire, others brought an end

to famines, and at least one spoke to dry bones that were in a moment's time turned into a living army. And still others installed and deposed kings, directed their armies, and even made declarations that changed the course of history. But John caught heaven's attention as no other prophet had done. He became known as the greatest born of a woman.

What was different about John's life and prophetic ministry? Consider first that Mark's Gospel specifically describes his ministry as the fulfillment of Isaiah's prophecy:

> Behold, *I send My messenger before Your face,* who will prepare Your way before You. The voice of one crying in the wilderness: "Prepare the way of the LORD; make His paths straight."
> —MARK 1:2–3, NKJV, EMPHASIS ADDED

John lived before the face of God—the ultimate place of favor and responsibility. He had an unusual grace for recognizing the presence of God, even before he was born. When Mary was pregnant with Jesus, she walked into a room to visit Elizabeth, who was pregnant with John. When Mary's greeting reached Elizabeth's ears, John leaped for joy while still in her womb.[1] Amazing—John was still what our culture calls a fetus (in order to ease their conscience about abortion). And that unborn child was able to recognize God's presence. Even more significant was John's ability to recognize the connection that the presence of Christ had to his assignment and eternal destiny. That reality brought great celebration to him, although he was not yet even born. Great joy is always available to anyone who connects with his or her eternal purpose.

Luke's Gospel records the early years of John's life for several reasons. Not only does it show us that John was in tune with the presence of God from the womb, indicating the potential for what would fully mature in his ministry, but it also makes a point that this capacity was something that had to be protected. Zacharias did not believe the words of the angel sent to him from God with the message of John's birth. Because of this, God made him mute for the entire pregnancy. His tongue loosened only after he responded in obedience to the command of the Lord in naming his child *John*.[2] This is very important, for "Death and life are in the power of the tongue" (Proverbs 18:21). Left unto himself while still in his state of unbelief, Zacharias could have killed with his words the very purpose of God in the promise given to them. Later, his words spoken in agreement with the will of God were the key to releasing John's destiny. John was also protected by Elizabeth, who concealed her pregnancy for five months after conception. In other words, only when her pregnancy was becoming inarguably evident did she go public. The implication is that John's exposure to the careless speech of others could have affected what God wanted to do.

Many would argue that God's purposes will be accomplished regardless of the speech of others. Perhaps. But why then does He want us to know the effect of our words if they have no effect at all? The five months in seclusion were probably sufficient for her to become strong enough in her own faith to withstand the *well-meaning curses* that people would probably make—things like, "Oh, aren't you a little old to be having a child? Isn't there a good chance that this child will be born with deformities or retardation?" Being hidden away gave her time to settle into her call and learn how to be unaffected by the careless concern of others. Only with faith and confidence regarding her own call could she become strong enough to steward the anointing on her unborn child correctly.

Perhaps her main reason for hiding for five months included one more great responsibility, to protect John from the words of others. In our Western culture it sounds strange to hear someone talk of the effect of our words on an unborn child. Yet, I remind you, it was the *greeting* from Mary, the mother of Jesus, that caused John to rejoice. Words brought joy to an unborn child. Did he understand them? No, I doubt that very much. But a child has amazing discernment that, unless he or she has parents who understand the way the spirit world works and have learned how to steward their child's anointing and gift, tends to get trampled on through life until that child can no longer discern. When the essence of Mary's words reached his undefiled heart, he rejoiced! Elizabeth was then filled with the Holy Spirit, enabling her to become a good steward of the gift that God had given her son until the time that he was able to watch over it himself.

In the story of John's birth we see a powerful illustration of partnering with the Lord in speech and action in order to steward the call of God on his life.

JOHN'S ASSIGNMENT

No prophet ever bore the responsibility that was given to John the Baptist. His assignment was not only to walk before the face of God; he was also *to prepare the way for the face of God to be revealed* for all to see. This was the moment that all the other prophets had longed to see. Now everything would change.

Picture a common scene of the old world: an army marching through a town, followed by their king being carried on the shoulders of his servants. Now picture the same scene, except this time it's an army of one, dressed in camel's hair, making crooked places straight with his prophetic declarations. He too is followed by a King, but this is the King of all kings. John would usher in the King's face of divine favor. His assignment was not only to prepare the way for the clearest *revelation* of God but also to prepare the way for an actual *manifestation* of the face of God—Jesus Christ. In Christ, that which had existed in types and shadows for centuries would be brought into the open.

While that is the most important assignment ever given to a man, his assignment was not only to make declarations. More needed to be done to insure that the intended manifestation was as clear as our Creator intended:

> The next day he saw Jesus coming to him and said, *"Behold, the Lamb of God* who takes away the sin of the world! This is He on behalf of whom I said, 'After me comes a Man who has a higher rank than I, for He existed before me.' *I did not recognize Him,* but so that He

might be manifested to Israel, I came baptizing in water." John testified saying, "*I have seen the Spirit descending as a dove out of heaven, and He remained upon Him. I did not recognize Him,* but He who sent me to baptize in water said to me, 'He upon whom you see the Spirit descending and remaining upon Him, this is the One who baptizes in the Holy Spirit.' I myself have seen, and have testified that this is the Son of God."

—JOHN 1:29–34, EMPHASIS ADDED

John made an amazing statement when he said, "I did not recognize Him." Jesus didn't stand out as the Son of God—until the Holy Spirit came upon Him and remained. Jesus, the face of God, wasn't noticed until the Spirit of God came upon Him. The wonderful Holy Spirit has been positioned to manifest the face of God—first upon Jesus, then through Jesus to the world.

A key thought for me in this whole story is found in the phrase, "He remained upon Him." This punchy prophetic declaration describes how Jesus did life: He walked through life in such a way that the dove of the Spirit would not be startled and leave. In Him we see a lifestyle that was crafted around the passion to host the presence of the Spirit of God. Being a person on whom the Holy Spirit can remain has a cost. (Cost in this context has nothing to do with works. It is passion for Him and a reverence for His presence where every move we make has Him in mind.)

Matthew's Gospel records the details of Jesus's baptism by John. At first John resisted Jesus for all the obvious reasons. He was not worthy to untie Jesus's shoes, let alone baptize Him. On top of that, Jesus was not a sinner and had no need of public repentance. Yet John obeyed—and then he witnessed one of the most amazing moments in history. Heaven opened, the Spirit of the living God descended upon the Son of man, and the Father spoke in affirmation to His Son. Here is the full account:

> Then Jesus arrived from Galilee at the Jordan coming to John, to be baptized by him. But John tried to prevent Him, saying, "I have need to be baptized by You, and do You come to me?" But Jesus answering said to him, "Permit it at this time; for in this way it is fitting for us to fulfill all righteousness." . . . After being baptized, Jesus came up immediately from the water; and behold, the heavens were opened, and he saw the Spirit of God descending as a dove and lighting on Him, and behold, a voice out of the heavens said, "This is My beloved Son, in whom I am well-pleased."
>
> —MATTHEW 3:13–17

Previous to this encounter, John had announced that Jesus would come with a different baptism than his, the baptism of the Holy Spirit and fire.[3] John was speaking of this baptism when he made the startling statement, "I need to be baptized by you." When Jesus came to be baptized by John it violated everything that John had thought about their different assignments. He knew that his role was to identify the Son of God and prepare people with a baptism of repentance from sin so that they could receive the revelation of the face of God in the Son. He also knew that the Son's role was to reveal this face through His baptism, the baptism of the Spirit. In his statement, we see that John's regard was not for his title or his role, but it was entirely for the One he served. John, the one who is called the greatest of those born of women, revealed his biggest need. He needed the baptism that Jesus offered—the baptism in the Holy Spirit and fire.

At the beginning of the chapter I referred to Jesus's statement that the least in the kingdom is greater than John—greater than the greatest born of women. If the people Jesus was referring to are those who are already in paradise, it's a moot point. Jesus didn't waste words. Rather He was giving a significant revelation about the kind of person that would be walking the earth not many days later—people born of the Spirit and baptized in the Spirit. It is in this context that John's confession, "I need to be baptized by You," makes sense. The one thing he, the greatest prophet of all, lacked is now available to every born-again believer. The baptism in the Spirit, a profound encounter with the face of God, adds the power of heaven to bring transformation to planet Earth. This baptism qualifies *the least in the kingdom to be greater than John*. It is a promise that is in effect now, to the degree we live in and manifest the King's domain.

THE ULTIMATE CONTROVERSY

When we realize that John lived before the face of God and that this face was revealed in Jesus Christ, specifically from the moment that He was clothed in power by the Holy Spirit, then the question that needs to be asked is, *what did this face look like?* What was the nature of God that Christ revealed? This topic would take many volumes of books to address properly. But if I had to pick one word to describe the nature of God revealed in Christ, it is that He is *good*.

I never realized how controversial the subject of the nature of God could be until I began teaching week after week that God is good, *always*. While most believers hold the belief as a theological value, especially because it is so stated in Nahum 1:7 and elsewhere, they struggle in light of the difficulties all around us. Many have abandoned the idea altogether, thinking it doesn't have any practical application. The hardest part is saying that He's *always* good. Some will say He is *mysteriously good*, which is about the same as saying He's good, but not as we think of goodness. This response doesn't help to clear up the confusion over the nature of God.

When we turn to the Scriptures we encounter similar apparent contradictions between the statement that God is always good and actual events in which He does not seem to be expressing goodness. While the Old Testament certainly contains revelations of God's compassion and love for people, it is also riddled with many incidents that seem to imply otherwise. To those who do not have a personal relationship with God, this especially appears to be the case. The Old Testament is filled with accounts of all kinds of tragedies and

> *If I had to pick one word to describe the nature of God revealed in Christ, it is that He is good.*

conflicts that God seemed to bring upon people because of their sin and rebellion. The Old Testament seems to portray God as being quite different from the God we see through Jesus Christ in the New Testament.

More specifically, in the New Testament Jesus works against the tragedies that are devouring people's lives and tries to bring restoration and healing. How many sick and diseased people came to Him and left afflicted and disappointed? How many times did Jesus actually say that the problem a person had was because God the Father was trying to teach a lesson that would ultimately make him more like Him? To how many diseased people did He try to explain that it just wasn't God's timing for them to be well? How many tormented people did He leave in that condition, saying, "This is the result of their choices. I would set them free if they really wanted to be free"? How many storms did Jesus bless? He not only lived differently from their common understanding of God; He lived in complete *contradiction* to their common understanding of God.

This striking distinction has eluded many. It has become common for believers to think God brings or allows sickness so that we will become more like Jesus. Today it is accepted for leaders to teach that God brings calamity because He knows it will draw us nearer to Him. If that line of thought were true, then mental hospitals and cancer wards would be glowing with God's manifest presence as all their patients would have drawn near to God and been transformed into the likeness of Jesus. Two thousand years ago all sickness was from the devil and healing was from God; today people teach that sickness is from God and those who pursue a healing ministry are from the devil (or out of balance, at best). How far we have fallen!

While it's true that believers can respond to disease and calamity with sacrificial acts of love and kindness, ministry should never be reduced to merely that. We are to be Christlike in loving service. But we have defined the responsibility of being like Jesus through this lens alone instead of by the way He dealt with such issues. Jesus stopped storms; He wasn't interested in just helping with the cleanup afterward. He resurrected the dead instead of conducting funerals. He healed the blind instead of training seeing-eye dogs.

Some have gone so far as to say that, like a good-cop-bad-cop scenario, the Father is the angry One and Jesus is the merciful side of God. Nothing could be further from the truth. Confusion over the nature of the persons of the Trinity has made us welcome deception in our ranks.

Most of those who embrace the idea that God is an angry Father do so in equal proportion to their inability to demonstrate His power. Powerlessness demands an explanation or a solution. Blaming God seems to be easier than it is to take responsibility and pursue an encounter with Him that changes our capabilities in ministry.

RECONCILING THE FATHER AND THE SON

One of the most important features of the gospel message is that the nature of the Father is perfectly seen in Jesus Christ. Jesus was a manifestation of the Father's nature. Whatever is thought to be in conflict between the Father in the Old Testament and the Son in the New Testament is in fact wrong. All inconsistencies in the revelation of the nature of God between the Old and New Testaments are cleared up in Jesus Christ. Jesus demonstrated the Father in everything He did. In short, Jesus is perfect theology:

> And He is the radiance of His glory and *the exact representation of His nature,* and upholds all things by the word of His power. When He had made purification of sins, He sat down at the right hand of the Majesty on high, having become as much better than the angels, as He has inherited a more excellent name than they.
>
> —HEBREWS 1:3–4, EMPHASIS ADDED

Some may ask, "What about Job?" I would respond, "I'm not a disciple of Job. I'm a disciple of Jesus. Job was the question, and Jesus is the answer." The entire Old Testament painted a picture of the problem so that it would be easy to recognize the answer when He came. If my study of Job does not take me to Jesus Christ as the answer, then I never understood Job. The Book of Job, along with all other questions about God's nature, are not meant to provide a revelation of God that would preempt the clear revelation of God through Jesus Christ.

For the believer, it is theologically immoral to allow an Old Testament revelation of God to cancel or contradict the perfect and clear manifestation of God in Jesus. I'm not denying that God displays anger and judgment in the Old Testament, as did Jesus to some degree, but by and large Jesus came with a display of extraordinary compassion. This is the revelation of God that believers are responsible to teach and model. This was made clear in Jesus's statement, "As the Father has sent Me, I also send you" (John 20:21).

The only justifiable model we have is Jesus Christ. The job description is fairly simple: heal the sick, raise the dead, cast out demons, and cleanse lepers.[4] If you say you are not gifted in such things, then I say, "Find out why." Most of what we need in life will be brought to us, but most of what we want we'll have to go and get. God has made these realities available. We must pursue them. These gifts are the overflow of the *face of God* encounter.

THE LORD'S PRAYER

I don't have answers to all the questions about the differences in the portrait of God throughout Scriptures. But I have found a wonderful key for life: it's best to live from what you know to be true in spite of the mysteries that you can't explain. I cannot afford to stumble over my questions when what I *do* understand demands a response and commitment. The portrait of God the Father, as seen in Jesus Christ, is wonderfully clear. He deserves the rest of my life as I learn how to imitate Him.

As previously stated, Jesus set aside His divinity, choosing instead to live as a man completely dependent on God. In doing so, He not only modeled a supernatural lifestyle, but He also illustrated that the ultimate quest is for the face of God. His lifestyle of both fasting and praying on the mountain throughout the night—a lifestyle He no doubt had established long before the Spirit descended upon Him—demonstrated His unquestionable priority to seek God's face.

To say that Jesus came both to manifest the face of God and illustrate the quest for His face may sound a little confusing, but both are true. Remember, Jesus modeled for us what it looked like to grow in favor with God as well as with man. The heavenly Father responded to His Son by giving an open heaven, which was followed by words of affirmation, saying, "This is My beloved Son in whom I am well pleased." It was in this encounter that the Father released the Holy Spirit upon His Son, enabling Him to manifest His face to the world.

It's best to live from what you know to be true in spite of the mysteries that you can't explain.

The Father, by the Holy Spirit, directed all that Jesus said and did. It was the intimacy that Jesus had with His heavenly Father that became the foundation for all the signs, wonders, and miracles performed in His three and a half years of earthly ministry.

As we saw in the last chapter, Ezekiel made the prophetic declaration, "I will not hide My face from them any longer, for

I will have poured out my Spirit on [them]" (Ezekiel 39:29). The face of God is revealed in the outpouring of the Holy Spirit. The outpouring of the Spirit also needed to happen to Jesus for Him to be fully qualified. This was His quest. Receiving this anointing qualified Him to be called the *Christ*, which means "anointed one." Without the experience there could be no title.

THE ULTIMATE DISAPPEARS

In John 17 we read Jesus's prayer about how He has fulfilled His assignment in ministry, saying, "I have glorified You...I have finished the work...I have manifested Your name...I have given them Your word...As You sent Me into the world, I also have sent them...The glory which You gave Me I have given them... I have declared to them Your name" (John 17:4, 6, 14, 18, 22, 26, NKJV). Clearly, Jesus's assignment was to put His Father's name, work, glory, and Word on display, particularly to this select group of disciples.

But then Jesus shocked His disciples when He told them He had to leave. Picture this—the face of God had come, and they had encountered Him and beheld His glory.[5] Now they were hearing that this experience, which had become the ultimate encounter with God imaginable, was to be taken away from them. To top it off, Jesus said it would actually be better if He left them. "It is to your advantage that I go away; for if I do not go away, the Helper will not come to you; but if I go, I will send Him to you" (John 16:7).

Jesus manifested the face of God to mankind. But it was only when He was taken away that He could release His experience to become their experience. And so He sent the Holy Spirit to come upon them. This meant that they could have their own encounter with God's face in a way that was not available through Jesus Himself. In other words, Jesus's experience was to become the normal experience of all who follow. This encounter brings us into the ultimate transformation, that we might become the ultimate transformers.

THE PRACTICAL SIDE OF GLORY

When Moses asked to see God's glory, God revealed His goodness.[6] The goodness of God is revolutionary in nature.

His goodness is not a token act of kindness but is instead a picture of God's overwhelming pursuit of humanity that He might show us His extreme love and mercy. People get stuck on God's ability to judge and forget that He is the One who looks for the opportunity to show mercy. Many of His own children live in ignorance regarding His goodness and therefore continually misrepresent Him. In fact, no matter how horrible a person's sin or life was, from the woman caught in adultery to the tormented man of Gaderene, Jesus

It is this single factor of being aware of personal need that enables someone to recognize that which God is doing in the earth.

revealed the face of God by showing mercy. These actions were never meant to be momentary displays of kindness so that in the twenty-first century God could finally punish people. His heart to forgive and show mercy is clear in the person of Jesus Christ. Jesus is the clearest manifestation of the face of God that mankind has ever seen.

Many will remind us that while God is good, He is still the judge of all. And that is true. But in Jesus's time that judgment was only directed at the people who claimed to know God but didn't know Him at all: the religious leaders. Jesus was a continual threat to their empire of selfishness built on religious service. They were good at rejection, punishment, and restriction, but they were clueless about the heart of God—the very one they claimed to know. They knew little about the boundless love of God and His passion for the freedom of all humanity.

At one time Jesus said to the Pharisees, "It is not those who are healthy who need a physician, but those who are sick; I did not come to call the righteous, but sinners" (Mark 2:17). The most spiritually diseased people on the planet were the religious leaders. Yet His statement did not make an impact on them because they lacked awareness of their personal need. They were lacking in the genuine righteousness that comes from a relationship with God. Harlots and tax collectors had a step up on the Pharisees simply because they were aware of their need. "Blessed are the *poor in spirit*, for theirs is the kingdom of heaven" (Matthew 5:3, emphasis added). But the Pharisees' lack of awareness of spiritual need disqualified them for the call of God to salvation.

Ironically, the greatest sinners were the ones who recognized who Jesus was when He came. The prostitutes, stargazers, tax collectors, and harlots all recognized Jesus as the Messiah. The ones most trained in Scripture were the ones who didn't recognize Him for who He was. It is this single factor of being aware of personal need that enables someone to recognize that which God is doing in the earth.

The awareness of deep personal need is also the setting where extraordinary faith grows. When there is no awareness of need, the opportunity to respond to God remains out of reach. For this reason, the Pharisees had no access to the realm that pleases God the most—faith. And faith moves God unlike any other thing.

CHAPTER 6

SETTING UP AN AMBUSH

*H*unger for God is one of the greatest signs of life a person can have. It reveals an inner awareness of the existence of greater destiny and personal fulfillment. Some people have a theological concept about God's presence being with them, but they are stuck with no true interaction or experience. We must press past intellectual awareness to hunger for heartfelt encounters that change and transform.

The desire itself is testimony that there is more, and the fact that we possess this desire to seek God should encourage us to pursue these encounters. It is nearly impossible to hunger for something that does not exist. I crave sweets only because sweet things exist. In the same way, my heart cries out for God because I was created to find complete fulfillment in Him alone. And the more I come to know Him, the more I become sure that He will be faithful to satisfy the desire He put in me.

One of Jesus's most important promises was given to His disciples just prior to His death. "He who loves Me... *I will* love him and *manifest Myself to him*" (John 14:21, NKJV, emphasis added). He promised that they would see Him again. This is clearly not merely a promise that they would see Him in heaven, because that was a given. It was also not a promise for these disciples only, but rather for all who love Him. (Otherwise we might think that this promise only referred to the appearance Jesus made to His disciples before He ascended.)

This promise was for every generation of believers, and it can mean nothing less than that He would make Himself conspicuous to us and that we would surely see Him again and again. We are not only to receive the Holy Spirit in power; we are also to see Jesus over and over again. That has to be the best of both worlds. God has given us these promises explicitly that we might seek Him with abandon, confident that He will be found by those who love Him and seek Him with all their hearts.

GOD LOOKS AT THE HEART

God reveals Himself to those who love Him. What kind of people are those who love Him? If we made a list of people in Scripture who illustrate what it looks like to love God, David would probably be at the top of the list. It's amazing to see what this love for God led him into.

When God sent the prophet Samuel to anoint the man He had chosen to replace King Saul, He explained to him that He didn't look on outward appearance but instead looked on the heart. It was from that perspective that David was chosen over his brothers, who were all better suited for greatness in the natural. Yet David's heart of passion for God attracted God to David. As a result, he was chosen to be king. While God is very capable of multitasking—of giving His undivided attention to each person on the planet all at the same time—He is drawn the most strongly to the ones whose hearts have been refined in their pursuit of Him.

God turns His face of favor toward those who will demonstrate character when no one is looking.

David's passion for God was first seen on the backside of a mountain while tending his father's sheep. In the quiet part of our day, when no one is looking, the true desires of our hearts can be seen. So it was with David. David was a skilled musician who wrote songs of worship to God. He did this long before this was a normal expression of worship. Up to this point in history, Israel had been instructed to offer the blood sacrifice to God as their basic worship expression. But there had been very little instruction about the sacrifice of thanksgiving and praise that could be given from the heart. David discovered that this was important to God as he pursued God. He learned that what really pleased God was the offering of a broken and contrite heart. And David was eager to give it. His zeal for God became evident as he gave himself to the privilege of worship and ministered directly to the Lord.

David embraced responsibility to watch over his father's sheep with equal zeal. (Many have passion for their life's goals and ambitions, but David was rightly directed.) When a lion and a bear attacked his father's sheep, he put his own life at risk to save them. Remember, he did this when no one was looking; it was not done so others would recognize him as a brave young man. It came out of his identity with God. He killed them both, and such courage and integrity set him up for the moment God allowed him to kill Goliath when everyone was looking. A private victory leads to a public victory and a corporate blessing, because God turns His face of favor toward those who will demonstrate character when no one is looking.

Many years after David's rule there arose another king. The prophet Elisha gave him instruction to strike the ground with arrows. The king followed his command and did so three times. The prophet became angry at his casual approach to the assignment and announced that if he would have struck the ground five or six times, he would have annihilated their enemies. But instead he would enjoy only three temporary victories. All of Israel would suffer the consequences of his passionless act. The sobering fact is this—leaders who lack passion cost everyone who follows. Not so with David. He endeared himself to God as a man of great passion—for God and for life.

The Striving Is Over

David's great love for God led him to discover the truth that God will be found by those who seek Him. A great command found in Psalms reveals one of King David's secrets in life. "Rest in the LORD and wait patiently for Him" (Psalm 37:7). The word *rest* used in this verse means one of two things, depending on the context. One is "to be still." That would be consistent with our use of the word in the English language. The other definition is rather fascinating, though. It means "to take a leisure walk." I think automatically of God and Adam walking in the Garden of Eden together in the cool of the day. This illustrates that true rest is found in a right relationship with God.

We know that all that was stolen because of Adam's sin is restored in the Last Adam, Jesus Christ. So, to *rest in the Lord* means basically that the obstacle to the relationship is removed and the striving is over. I don't need to fight to gain God's attention. I already have His favor and will walk favorably with Him in the adventure of a developing personal relationship. All of this is provided for in the gift of salvation. It is amazing to realize that David discovered this power of waiting on God while under the old covenant.

Many people work for God's attention and favor instead of learning to work with God because of His favor. They become so exhausted working *for* Him that there's little strength left to work *with* Him when He opens the doors for significant service. At the root of this problem is ignorance about Christ's acceptance of each of us, and it has cost us dearly. We work so hard to gain favor from God that we might be accepted, when all the while that's the opposite of how life works in the kingdom.

Because Jesus is my righteousness, I am already accepted. From that acceptance comes favor, and that favor gives birth to authentic Christlike works of service. I serve *from* Him, not merely *for* Him. This simple progression really is the key to ministry. This was the model that Jesus gave us. He only did what He saw His Father do and said what He heard His Father say.

The classic example of this is the story of Mary and Martha. Mary chose to sit at Jesus's feet while Martha chose to work in the kitchen.[1] Mary sought to please Him by being with Him while Martha tried to please Him through service. When Martha became jealous, she asked Jesus to tell Mary to help her in the kitchen. Most servants want to degrade the role of the friend to feel justified in their works-oriented approach to God. Jesus's response is important to remember: "Mary has chosen the better part." Martha was making a meal that Jesus never ordered. Doing more for God is the method servants use to get God's attention that they might

> *I serve from Him, not merely for Him. This simple progression really is the key to ministry.*

increase in favor. A friend has a different focus entirely: they enjoy the favor they have and use it to spend time with their master.

To say we need both Marys and Marthas is to miss the point entirely. And it simply isn't true. Perhaps you've heard it said that nothing would ever get done if we didn't have any Marthas. That too is a lie. That teaching comes mostly from Marthas who are intimidated by the lifestyle of Marys. Mary wasn't a nonworker. Rather she was beginning to be like her Master, who only did what He saw the Father do. Jesus was talking, so Mary set aside other distractions and sat down to listen. She didn't get caught up in making the sandwiches that Jesus didn't order. She was learning that working from His presence is much more effective than working for His presence.

ANOTHER LOOK AT WAITING

One of the problems that we have in our study of Scripture is that we tend to interpret things through our own experience and culture. *Waiting patiently for God* is a great example. For most of us, this statement brings a passive image to mind. Many have found this to be a way to blame God for their spiritual laziness: "Oh, we're just waiting on God." And they've done so for years, wasting valuable time, hoping that God will invade their lives with some sense of significance.

However, waiting on God is not a passive, "lean-back-in-the-recliner" attitude that says, "When God wants to touch me, He knows my address." There are still people who sit back and say,

"Boy, I hear God is doing great things all over the world. I just wish He would move in my life or my church. I wish He'd do something great in my city." This kind of *waiting on God* attitude is not the one we see in the Scriptures.

This Hebrew word *patiently* is in the Bible fifty-three times. Four times it is defined as "waiting patiently," "to wait," "waiting," or "waited." Forty-nine times it is defined as "writhing in pain, as in childbirth" or "whirling in the air in dance." The characteristics involved in childbirth and the dance give us the needed insight on how to practice waiting patiently on God. We could never watch someone involved in giving birth to a child or dancing skillfully to music and think that they were passive about what they were doing. Passion is the nature of both expressions. And passion leads the way in waiting patiently on God.

In our culture, *patience* connotes the attitude expressed by words such as these: "I'm just going to put up with this annoyance for another day, because I'm patient." That's not the biblical patience David was talking about. If *waiting patiently* is seen in the activity of leaping and whirling about in a dance, then the person who is waiting will have to be incredibly focused. Their love for the dance takes them into a discipline that brings out creative excellence. Dancers must be intensely focused on their bodies, the music, and where they're going to land. At minimum, without that much-needed discipline and focus, injuries would be certain.

The same kind of intense, all-consuming focus characterizes giving birth to a child in the midst of incredible pain. I had the privilege of being present for the birth of each of my children. When my wife was giving birth to our third child, Leah, I made the mistake of turning my head toward someone else in the room during a contraction. I quickly discovered that it was definitely the wrong time to have done so. When I turned my attention elsewhere, it affected her ability to keep her focus, which was essential in keeping her writhing in pain at a minimum. I made this mistake when my wife needed my help the most. Her death grip on my arm helped me to return to my senses and realize that there was really only one person who should have all my attention at that moment.

There's something about both the dance and giving birth that requires incredible resolve to reach an intended end. This is waiting patiently for God. It has intense focus, disciplined resolve, and a conviction that *nothing else will satisfy*. God is attracted to people who have that kind of tenacity and who are not satisfied with inferior things.

THERE'S MORE

David uses another word to expand his portrait of our waiting on God. "But those who *wait* for the LORD, they will inherit the land" (Psalm 37:9, emphasis added). Here the word *wait* means, "to lie in wait," as in setting up an ambush. That is about as far away from the passive definition as can be imagined. It is almost militant, still carrying the discipline of the intense focus mentioned earlier, but along with an eager pursuit. Isaiah expressed the same idea: "And I will wait for the LORD who is hiding His face from the house of Jacob; I will even look eagerly for Him" (Isaiah 8:17).

If I want to hunt deer, I won't set up an ambush on Wall Street in New York City or in the middle of the Pacific Ocean. To set up an ambush with any hope of success, I must do so in areas that deer frequent. But many do not realize that the same is true of waiting on God. There are many who need a miracle, but they won't go across town to a church where miracles are common. We play a mental game of pride when we refuse to humble ourselves and go to lie in wait in the places that God frequents.

Now, please don't stumble over the concept of ambushing God as though it violates His sovereignty—He is the One who has promised to be found by us if we seek Him with all of our hearts. And He is the One who said He would make Himself conspicuous as we pursue Him. This is His idea. It is our test to see if we believe Him enough to *look eagerly* for Him. God is looking for someone who will get out of his or her routine and set up an ambush.

Some people get really upset when they see believers traveling all over the world because those believers have heard that God is doing something significant in a particular place. Their reasoning: "God is everywhere. Seek Him where you are, and He will come to you." Similarly, preachers with little breakthrough anointing will say, "You're not supposed to follow signs. They are supposed to follow you!" That looks good on paper and carries a measure of truth. But as I said in the first chapter, if signs are not following you, you had better follow them until they follow you. Remember, signs point to a greater reality. We are not to follow them for their own sake but because they lead us to the One who created them. Getting in touch with Him is how we become those whom signs follow. While they may not realize it, many who travel anywhere at any cost just because of their hunger for God are doing exactly what David taught about waiting on God. They go to where He is working and lie in wait, anticipating His every move, looking for the chance to reach out and touch God.

Matthew described such an extraordinary act in the story of a woman who had been hemorrhaging for twelve years. She positioned herself in such a way that she was able to touch the hem of Jesus's garment as He was making His way down the road.[2] It was no easy feat. There were large crowds of people pressing in upon Him. Yet she was the only one who saw the dimension of heaven that He was carrying and touched Him in a way that put a demand on the anointing of the Holy Spirit that was resident in Him. That is the kind of faith that pleases God. It is the classic example of how God welcomes being *ambushed.*

FOLLOWING IN JACOB'S FOOTSTEPS

There are several notable characters in Scripture who illustrate clearly what it looks like to wait on God with this intense focus and passion. I want to consider three of them, beginning with Jacob.

Jacob, despite his deep personal issues with deception and manipulation, had an intense desire for the blessing of the Lord.

He would not be well liked today by those who criticize the ones who are constantly looking for God's blessing. He simply wanted God to be real in his life. His pursuit culminated when he had to face what he believed would be the most dangerous situation of his life—meeting his brother Esau for the first time after obtaining Esau's birthright and stealing his blessing. The circumstances were desperate—he believed that his brother wanted vengeance. Not everyone turns to God in desperate circumstances. Some might throw up a last-ditch prayer, but few take the step of grabbing onto God as their only hope and holding on for dear life until His answer comes. Jacob did this, and it was this focused passion and faith that attracted the Lord to him. In response God sent an angel to make a visit.[3]

> Then Jacob was left alone, and a man wrestled with him until daybreak. When he saw that he had not prevailed against him, he touched the socket of his thigh; so the socket of Jacob's thigh was dislocated while he wrestled with him. Then he said, "Let me go, for the dawn is breaking." But he said, "*I will not let you go unless you bless me.*"
>
> —GENESIS 32:24–26, EMPHASIS ADDED

In response to his persistence, Jacob received a name change. This name change reflected the character change that had occurred with him in his pursuit of the blessing. His name was changed from *Jacob* ("deceiver") to *Israel* ("God strives"). He was injured in this encounter with God, and he limped for the rest of his life—that was the cost for his persistence. Such resolve always has a cost:

> So he said to him, "What is your name?" And he said, "Jacob." He said, "Your name shall no longer be Jacob, but Israel; for you have striven with God and with men and have prevailed." Then Jacob asked him and said, "Please tell me your name." But he said, "Why is it that you ask my name?" And he blessed him there. So Jacob named the place Peniel, for he said, "*I have seen God face to face,* yet my life has been preserved." Now the sun rose upon him just as he crossed over Penuel, and he was limping on his thigh.
>
> —Genesis 32:27–31, emphasis added

I guess that when you realize you survived looking at the face of God, surviving an angry brother seems easy. Significantly, when Jacob later met Esau and found favor with him, he said, "No, please, if I have now found favor in your sight, then receive my present from my hand, inasmuch as I have seen your face as though I had seen the face of God, and you were pleased with me" (Genesis 33:10, NKJV). This episode clearly reveals the power of the blessing and favor that came upon Jacob's life after his encounter and name change—his brother treated him like a completely different person.

But it was the quest for God's face that started the change in Jacob. His life is a great reminder that one does not need to be perfect to begin this journey. In fact, it is this quest that perfects.

The ultimate encounter in life was given to Jacob. His conclusion was, "I have seen God face to face, yet my life has been preserved." It saddens me to see the great number of people who feel they have to clean up their lives before they meet the only One who cleanses. It's an impossible task that creates pressure and striving for a relationship with God. Just being able to follow, without distraction, our hearts' desire to know God—that's what causes more transformation than any list of rules found in religion.

FOLLOWING IN ELISHA'S FOOTSTEPS

Elisha provides another great example of waiting patiently, and, like Jacob, he illustrates that the capacity to wait is the thing that determines whether we will experience spiritual breakthroughs that release a new measure of power and authority in our lives.

Elisha spent years in training as Elijah's assistant, and eventually the time came for the Lord to take Elijah home. The whole prophetic community, as well as Elisha, seemed to know the day on which this was to occur. Strangely, on this day it also seemed that Elijah tried to ditch his spiritual son at every turn. But Elisha followed Elijah like a shadow and wouldn't let him out of his sight. When Elijah asked him what he could do for him before he was taken, Elisha shot for the moon. He said, "Please, let a double portion of your spirit be upon me" (2 Kings 2:9). Elijah's personal experience was already the high watermark for all prophets. What Elisha asked for was very difficult because of the price involved. The Lord showed Elijah how Elisha would be tested to see if he had what it would take to carry a double portion of Elijah's anointing.

This lesson is huge. Gifts of the Spirit rest best on the fruit of the Spirit. That's why the Bible says that faith actually works through love. The word for works or working in Galatians 5:6 is *energeo*, from which we get our word *energy*. In other words, *faith is energized through love*. Gifts are energized by character. And without the energy of character flowing through our lives, we won't be able to exercise the gifts consistently and with excellence. The anointing of the Spirit from which these gifts flow is given to bless and release the reality of heaven to Earth. But it is weighty.

Only integrity joined with passion could enable Elisha to carry a double measure of Elijah's anointing. The test was simple but not easy. Elijah said, "You have asked a hard thing. Nevertheless, if you see me when I am taken from you, it shall be so for you; but if not, it shall not be so" (2 Kings 2:10). It is interesting to note that the Lord chose to test Elisha in the very thing he was already doing—keeping his eyes on his master. Elisha was probably already dogging Elijah's steps to the point where Elijah couldn't go to the bathroom without Elisha being present. God simply arranged the circumstances in order to see whether what he was doing out of instinct had enough force of character behind it to be sustained in spite of the kind of distractions he would face, should he be entrusted with a double portion. Here we see what kind of distractions they would be:

As they were going along and talking, behold, there appeared
a chariot of fire and horses of fire which separated the two of
them. And Elijah went up by a whirlwind to heaven.

—2 KINGS 2:11

As Elisha kept his assignment to watch Elijah, the unexpected happened. A chariot of fire came down out of heaven. The chariot didn't take Elijah to heaven, as some have surmised. The Scriptures tell us that Elijah was actually taken up in a whirlwind. So what was the chariot of fire for? It was the test. If Elisha were to carry a double portion of Elijah's anointing, it would mean that there would be many unusual signs and wonders surrounding his life. Could Elisha keep his eyes on his assignment (Elijah in this case), even when the activities of heaven invaded the atmosphere? Could he anchor his heart into the will of God and not be pulled away by the wonder of his gift? Most of us would have failed this test. After all, how could we go wrong by putting our attention on God's activities? But Elisha's quest for the double portion anointing was fulfilled in this encounter, for Elisha wouldn't be distracted by his own gift and anointing.

God desires to release gifts to us more than we desire to receive them. He is just too merciful to release gifts upon us that He would have to judge us for later because we failed to carry them with integrity. However, we must also realize that even when we pass a particular character test and are entrusted with a greater measure of anointing, we have not *arrived*. We all know those who have begun well in the race of faith and have been entrusted with a wonderful anointing to bless the body of Christ, only to fall later in life. This is a lifelong race that we are running, and God works in every part of it to groom us to carry what He wants to give us, both for this life and the next.

Following in Jesus's Footsteps

Our key to running a successful race is the same as Elisha's. As Hebrews tells us, the key is to fix our eyes on our Master. We are successful when we fix our eyes on Jesus precisely because He is the One who has run the race ahead of us. He had to undergo the same tests of character that Elisha faced and that we must face. He modeled success for us by keeping *His* eyes fixed on the Father at all times. Like Elisha's ultimate test, Jesus's test required Him to keep His focus in the face of separation from His Father.

In His journey to the cross, Jesus demonstrated the ultimate example of the kind of passionate focus that we've been considering. He set His face toward Jerusalem, knowing He was about to die: "Nevertheless I must journey on today and tomorrow and the next day; for it cannot be that a prophet would perish outside of Jerusalem" (Luke 13:33).

It's important to realize that Jesus pursued this focus without any support from those closest to Him. He carefully took the time to prepare His disciples for His death. But no matter how much He talked with them, they didn't understand. Not only did they not comprehend the issue of the cross, they opposed the little they did understand. At one point Peter actually rebuked Jesus for His repeated references to His personal death.

His death was to be unlike any other in all of history. Jesus Christ was without sin, yet He would bear the sins of all mankind from all time. The weight of such a burden is beyond comprehension. In His death the Son of God was separated from His Father for the first and only time. This separation is another unimaginably difficult experience that Jesus embraced for our sakes.

And yet we read that Jesus did what He did "for the joy set before Him" (Hebrews 12:2). His eyes were fixed on something beyond the cross—the reconciliation of many sons to His Father. Likewise, in the race of each of our lives, God has set a joy before us, and it is the joy of sharing in this reconciliation that Christ has purchased for us. But as we become people who can drink of that joy in its fullness, we may pass through testing and sacrifice when it feels like God has turned His face from us.

It is a precious and vital secret to discover that, for those who seek the face of God, these moments are actually God's invitations into greater power and intimacy.

ANOTHER PARADOX

We live in an hour when the face of God is being revealed in a wonderful outpouring of the Holy Spirit. *There's no limit to what is possible for one person, church, city, or nation to experience.* The Bible points to what has been made available, but how, when, or how much of it can be accessed has never been defined for us. Boundaries have never been set. While the glory of God in its fullness would kill us, there are measures of His presence that have been enjoyed by people in the past that far surpass what we now experience. It is my personal conviction that God has made available to us whatever measure of His glory our bodies can handle.

It may seem like a strange thing to encourage people to go after something in God with reckless abandon and in the same breath to exhort them to rest. But somehow it's the unique combination of those two things that define our challenge in this hour. This is the "rest that pursues." What God has done for me is so far beyond my wildest dreams. In one sense I could live in this place with God forever because He is so completely satisfying, yet being with Him stirs up dreams and passions that won't allow me to be stationary. There is so much at stake. I am alive for more!

We were born to live in the glory of God.

BE STILL AND EXPERIENCE GOD

I love the privilege of spending time with God—the more the better. Being still before Him is an often-underrated activity by those of us who like to accomplish and achieve things in prayer for the King and His kingdom.

This is how it looks for me. Sometimes I'll take just a few minutes in the middle of a workday for His pleasure. I get before the Lord and say something to this effect, "God, I'm here, but I'm not going to ask for anything or perform in any way for You. I'm just going to sit here simply as an object of Your love and let You love me." This is a big deal for me, because my usual prayer time is about 75 percent worship and 25 percent petition. Not doing stuff is sometimes hard. Sometimes when I enter that place of rest I get a picture of Him pouring a honey-colored oil all over me as a symbol of His love. It's an overwhelming picture of drowning in His love. Something wonderful begins to happen as He awakens every part of my life to His presence.

David said, "My soul thirsts for You, my flesh yearns for You" (Psalm 63:1). Think about this—before it was possible to be born again through the blood of Jesus, David said that his body actually hungered for God. It is possible to be so drenched in the glory of God through a lifestyle of worship that our bodies discover one of the great purposes for which they were created. We were born to live in the glory of God.[4] Whether it is five minutes or five hours, taking the time with God outside of the need for Christian performance is one of the most important decisions we can make.

THE CREATIVE MOMENT

When I sit before the Lord for this time of inactivity, I often remember things that must be done or ideas that will be good for my life or ministry. In my younger years I thought that this was always the devil trying to distract me from my time with God. But as I get older I realize that God is merely showing me that He is concerned about whatever concerns me. Time with Him releases a creativity that is paramount to fulfilling our assignment in life.

I now bring a pen and paper with me into that time with God. As ideas come I give thanks to God and write them down. By doing so I don't have to try to remember what God has said, but I can return my attention to Him. Not having the pressure to remember details releases us into a creative process. In this kind of prayer time I don't go before Him to get answers and directions. I am there simply to experience His love. But I have found that in that place of communion and love it is His pleasure to give revelation that satisfies our hearts. I just don't want anything to become the chariot that pulls me away from my opportunity to delight myself in the Lord. So I receive what He's giving me and then turn my attention back to the Giver Himself.

THE NECESSARY FRUIT

As I've stated, we will need to develop the capacity to sustain great passion and focus if we are going to become those who set up ambushes for God. There's a word in Scripture that describes this capacity: it is the word *self-control*. Self-control is first and foremost a fruit of the Spirit, which means that you can only get it through intimacy with Him. The fruit of our lives is not something that we work to produce; it is merely the evidence of whatever we spiritually commune with. Self-control in our lives is the evidence of the Holy Spirit's control and influence over us.

There are many people in the world who appear to be very self-controlled because they have very disciplined lives in certain areas. Religion offers plenty of ways to control our behavior, as do popular psychology, prescription drugs, and diets. But the practice of these disciplines fails to bring people to the place where the qualities of righteousness, peace, and joy in the Holy Spirit are continually present in their lives.

In contrast, those who are the most fruitful in the Spirit are not necessarily those who make a first impression of being very controlled and disciplined. If you get to know them, you will find that they are indeed disciplined, but that *discipline* is in fact an inadequate factor for measuring their success in life. It's like coming into the home of a proverbial loving couple and describing the husband as disciplined for going to work and the wife as disciplined for keeping the house clean and cooking dinner. They would probably reply that discipline has nothing to do with it—if they are disciplined, it is simply the fruit of their love and commitment to each other.

Likewise, the center of the Christian life is passion for God, and it is this passion that defines the boundaries of our lives. Self-control is the by-product of living in covenant with God. To demonstrate the character trait of true self-control, one must be able to illustrate what it looks like to live in perfect harmony with the values of the Spirit of God. We also show self-control in the way we protect our connection with God from other influences that could distract and dissuade us. But self-control is not only the ability to say no to all the options and voices that are contrary to the values of the kingdom of God. It is also the ability to say yes to something so completely that all other voices and values are silenced. Jesus demonstrated this best of all. He set

His face to go to Jerusalem and die. Nothing could distract Him from His purpose.

The same challenge is yours: set your face toward His purposes, and you will experience the greatest privilege known to humanity. Set your face, and you'll see His face.

CHAPTER 7

NEVER the SAME AGAIN

Throughout history there have been great numbers of people who refused to settle for whatever had become the norm. We applaud political leaders for being this way, and the same is true for innovators in education and entertainment. The leaders of business and especially technology and medicine attract great accolades from society for breaking out of the confines of past achievements. No doubt this is due in large part to the fact that their breakthroughs bring such benefit to the masses.

Yet new ideas are threatening: we tend to want to keep a distance from those who push the edge. The ideas that end up lasting the longest have usually been rejected first. Then they were tolerated, and eventually they are accepted.

Spiritual leaders who live on the edge as pioneers suffer the same conflict. They are also the ones most likely to be rejected at first. Opponents will often do most anything to silence the voice of one who says there is more. Feeling good about ourselves has become such an idol that many have become blind to the prophetic edge of the Scriptures. But some won't settle for what presently exists because they see how much more is available, as illustrated in the life of Jesus.

> *Today there is a new breed of believer. They may look quite different from each other, but they are known by their love and faith.*

Jesus's life demonstrates that there is more. And to pull us into our destiny, He said, "Greater works than these he will do; because I go to the Father" (John 14:12). It's hard to imagine, but Jesus declared that there would be a generation that would rise *above* His high watermark.

The stories of many such revolutionaries are recorded in Scripture. Others are recorded in various books of historical merit, giving us the testimonial record that God is in fact the same yesterday, today, and forever.

We are in the throes of change; a reformation will impact society on all fronts. This is happening largely because today there is a new breed of believer. They may look quite different from each other, but they are known by their love and faith. They just won't settle for what has been. While there is great admiration for those who have gone before, this group won't stop long enough to build them a monument or memorial. In fact, this generation knows that the best way to honor past accomplishments is by building on top of their breakthroughs.

THE VOICE OF HISTORY

It would be easy to make an entire book out of the testimonies of face-to-face encounters with God. Some of our most notable heroes of the faith had moments in which God invaded their lives in ways that were often unique, sometimes hard to believe. Their lives were changed dramatically, often in equal proportion to the strangeness of their encounter. Yet all of them were able to manifest an aspect of heaven throughout the remainder of their lives and to blaze a trail for future believers.

In the following section I have selected a handful of stories of some who made their mark on history. These revivalists are personal heroes, of which only one is alive today. They helped to shape the course of church history, which in turn shaped the course of world history. Yet all of their experiences are but a drop in the bucket of what is being released right now around the world.

Read these stories of divine encounters and their fruit. Hunger in the same way that they did. And then watch how God chooses to manifest Himself as the almighty God in your life.

Evan Roberts

Evan Roberts was the spark plug of the great Welsh revival of 1904–1906. During this time, more than one hundred thousand souls were saved, and a complete transformation of a nation took place. But even more significant was the fact that this move of God sparked the Azusa Street revival that has since gone all over the world.

Evan had a series of unusual experiences with God, including a number of face-to-face encounters. He described these in an interview with W. T. Stead, the editor of the British newsletter "Review of Reviews." That interview is quoted in Stead's book *The Story of the Welsh Revival*, written in 1905.

> For a long, long time, I was much troubled in my soul and my heart by thinking over the failure of Christianity...but that night, after I had been in great distress praying about this, I went to sleep, and at 1 am in the morning suddenly I was wakened up...and found myself with unspeakable joy and awe in the very presence of the Almighty God. And for the space of four hours I was privileged to speak face to face with Him, as a man speaks face to face with a friend. At 5 am it seemed to me as if I again returned to earth....And it was not only that morning, but every morning for three or four months....I felt it and it seemed

to change all my nature, and I saw things in a different light, and I knew that God was going to work in the land, and not in this land only, but in all the world.[1]

John G. Lake

John G. Lake was a wealthy insurance salesman who was touched by God in an extraordinary way. Day and night, earnestly and at great length, he sought more of the Holy Spirit.

Lake had an early experience in which he felt what he called "Waves of Holy Glory" by which he "was lifted into a new realm of God's presence and power. After this, answers to prayer were frequent and miracles of healing occurred from time to time. I felt myself on the borderland of a great spiritual realm, but was unable to enter in fully, so my nature was not satisfied with the attainment."[2]

In response, he pursued God's face more and more, dedicating certain hours of the day to prayer and maintaining communion with God's Spirit as he conducted his daily business. Almost every evening after his day's business was completed, Lake preached and ministered. He also met with a group of like-minded friends. Together, they were determined to "pray through" to their goal— a complete baptism of the Holy Spirit, as they believed the early disciples had received it, with signs following.

Lake said to the Lord, "God, if you will baptize me in the Holy Spirit, and give me the power of God, nothing shall be permitted to stand between me and a hundred-fold obedience."[3]

One day, the Lord said to him, "Be patient until autumn," and Lake knew his prayers were being heard. One afternoon that fall, a fellow minister asked Lake to accompany him to the home of a woman who had requested prayers for healing. For ten years this woman had been in a wheelchair because of inflammatory rheumatism. As his friend spoke with the lady to prepare her for prayer, Lake sat across the large room in a low chair. There, he had a powerful encounter with God:

> My soul was crying out to God in a yearning too deep for words, when suddenly it seemed to me that I had passed under a shower of warm tropical rain, which was not falling upon me but through me. My spirit and soul and body, under this influence, was soothed into such a deep still calm as I had never known. My brain, which had always been so active, became perfectly still. An awe of the presence of God settled over me. I knew it was God.
>
> Some moments passed; I do not know how many. The Spirit said, "I have heard your prayers, I have seen your tears. You are now baptized in the Holy Spirit." Then currents of power began to rush through my being from the crown of my head to the soles of my feet. The shocks of power increased in rapidity and voltage. As these currents of power would pass through me, they seemed to come upon my head, rush through my body and through my feet into the floor. The power was so great that my body began to vibrate intensely so that I believe if I had not

been sitting in such a deep low chair I might have fallen upon the floor.[4]

At that point, his friend, not noticing the state he was in, invited Lake to come to help him pray. Lake could hardly walk, he was trembling so violently. While his friend continued to kneel down in front of the woman's wheelchair, Lake simply touched her head lightly (so as not to jar her with his trembling), and he felt "currents of holy power" pass through his body. He knew she felt it too, even though she didn't say anything.

> My friend who had been talking to her in his great earnestness had been kneeling as he talked to her. He arose saying, "Let us pray that the Lord will now heal you." As he did so he took her by the hand. At the instant their hands touched, a flash of dynamic power went through my person and through the sick woman, and as my friend held her hand the shock of power went through her hand into him. The rush of power into his person was so great that it caused him to fall on the floor. He looked up at me with joy and surprise, and springing to his feet said, "Praise the Lord, John, Jesus has baptized you in the Holy Ghost!"
>
> Then he took the crippled hand, that had been set for so many years. The clenched hands opened and the joints began to work, first the fingers, then the hand and the wrist, then the elbow and shoulder.[5]

Lake himself was thrilled at the inexpressible peace and joy that flooded his inner being. He felt that truly the Spirit had imparted to him "a well of water springing up into everlasting life" (John 4:14, KJV). God's love poured through him. He saw people as lost sheep, and the passionate desire of his soul became the proclamation of the salvation message of Jesus, accompanied by powerful healing and blessing.

Lake's life was forever changed. He left the business world to pursue the lifestyle of signs and wonders, from which came one of the most notable healing ministries the world has ever known. He moved to Chicago in 1904 to receive training from the healing evangelist John Alexander Dowie. It was a time of great heart cleansing, during which the strength of Lake's spiritual gifts increased, especially the gift of healing.

After pastoring a church for a short time in Indianapolis, Lake moved his family to South Africa in 1908, where in a period of five years he planted 625 churches, raised up 1,250 local pastors, and saw 1,000,000 people converted to Jesus Christ.[6]

The pace was so intense, however, that his wife died. So in 1913, Lake returned to the United States with his seven children, where he remarried and undertook a traveling ministry. Two of his trips to the Pacific Northwest, to Spokane, Washington, and Portland, Oregon, resulted in the establishment of the "healing rooms" for which Lake is best known today. At one time, Spokane was declared "the healthiest city in the United States," after one hundred thousand verifiable healings had occurred over a five-year period. People traveled from far and wide to receive God's touch in one of the healing rooms.[7]

Charles Finney

Charles Finney was a lawyer who became a revivalist. The experience he had with God changed everything about his life, enabling him to bring about great transformation to the nation. Here is the story in his own words:

> By evening we got the books and furniture adjusted; and I made up, in an open fire-place, a good fire, hoping to spend the evening alone. Just at dark Squire W——, seeing that everything was adjusted, bade me good-night and went to his home. I had accompanied him to the door; and as I closed the door and turned around my heart seemed to be liquid within me. All my feelings seemed to rise and flow out; and the utterance of my heart was, "I want to pour my whole soul out to God." The rising of my soul was so great that I rushed into the room back of the front office to pray.
>
> There was no fire, and no light, in the room; nevertheless it appeared to me as if it were perfectly light. As I went in and shut the door after me, it seemed as if I met the Lord Jesus Christ face to face. It did not occur to me that it was wholly a mental state. On the contrary it seemed to me that I saw him as I would see any other man. He said nothing, but looked at me in such a manner as to break me right down at his feet. I have always since regarded this as a most remarkable state of mind; for it seemed that he

stood before me, and I fell down at his feet and poured out my soul to him. I wept aloud like a child, and made such confessions as I could with my choked utterance.

I must have continued in this state for a good while; but my mind was too much absorbed with the interview to recollect anything that I said. But I know, as soon as my mind became calm, I returned to the front office, and found that the fire that I had made of large wood was nearly burned out. But as I turned and was about to take a seat by the fire, I received a mighty baptism of the Holy Ghost. Without any expectation of it, without ever having the thought in my mind that there was any such thing for me, without any recollection that I had ever heard the thing mentioned by any person in the world, the Holy Spirit descended upon me in a manner that seemed to go through me, body and soul. I could feel the impression, like a wave of electricity, going through and through me. Indeed it seemed to come in waves and waves of liquid love; for I could not express it in any other way. It seemed like the very breath of God. I can recollect distinctly that it seemed to fan me, like immense wings.

No words can express the wonderful love that was shed abroad in my heart. I wept aloud with joy and love; and I do not know but I should say, I literally bellowed out the unutterable gushings of my heart. These waves came over me, and over me, and over me, one after the other, until I recollect I cried out, "I shall die if these waves continue to pass over me." I said, "Lord, I cannot bear any more;" yet I had no fear of death.

How long I continued in this state I do not know. But it was late in the evening when a member of my choir came to see me. He was a member of the church. He found me in this state of loud weeping, and said, "Mr. Finney, what ails you?" I could make him no answer for some time. He then said, "Are you in pain?" I gathered myself up as best I could, and replied, "No, but so happy that I cannot live."

He left the office, and in a few minutes returned with one of the elders of the church, whose shop was nearly across the way from our office. This elder was a very serious man; and in my presence had been very watchful, and I had scarcely ever seen him laugh. He asked me how I felt, and I began to tell him. Instead of saying anything, he fell into a most spasmodic laughter. It seemed as if it was impossible for him to keep from laughing from the very bottom of his heart.

There was a young man in the neighborhood who was preparing for college, with whom I had been very intimate. Our minister, as I afterward learned, had repeatedly talked with him on the subject of religion, and warned him against being misled by me. He informed him that I was a very careless young man about religion; and he thought that if he associated much with me his mind would be diverted, and he would not be converted.

After I was converted, and this young man was converted, he told me that he had said to Mr. Gale several times, when he had admonished him about associating so much with me, that my conversations had often affected him more, religiously, than his preaching. I had, indeed, let out my feelings a good deal to this young man.

But just at this time when I was giving an account of my feelings to this elder of the church, and to the other member who was with him, this young man came into the office. I was sitting with my back toward the door, and barely observed that he came in. He listened with astonishment to what I was saying, and the first I knew he partly fell upon the floor, and cried out in the greatest agony of mind, "Do pray for me!" The elder of the church and the other member knelt down and began to pray for him; and when they had prayed, I prayed for him myself. Soon after this they all retired and left me alone.

The question then arose in my mind, "Why did Elder B—— laugh so? Did he not think that I was under a delusion, or crazy?" This suggestion brought a kind of darkness over my mind; and I began to query with myself whether it was proper for me—such a sinner as I had been—to pray for that young man. A cloud seemed to shut in over me; I had no hold upon anything in which I could rest; and after a little while I retired to bed, not distressed in mind, but still at a loss to know what to make of my present state. Notwithstanding the baptism I had received, this temptation so obscured my view that I went to bed without feeling sure that my peace was made with God.

I soon fell asleep, but almost as soon awoke again on account of the great flow of the love of God that was in my heart. I was so filled with love that I could not sleep. Soon I fell asleep again, and awoke in the same manner.

When I awoke, this temptation would return upon me, and the love that seemed to be in my heart would abate; but as soon as I was asleep, it was so warm within me that I would immediately awake. Thus I continued till, late at night, I obtained some sound repose.

When I awoke in the morning the sun had risen, and was pouring a clear light into my room. Words cannot express the impression that this sunlight made upon me. Instantly the baptism that I had received the night before returned upon me in the same manner. I arose upon my knees in the bed and wept aloud with joy, and remained for some time too much overwhelmed with the baptism of the Spirit to do anything but pour out my soul to God. It seemed as if this morning's baptism was accompanied with a gentle reproof, and the Spirit seemed to say to me, "Will you doubt?" "Will you doubt?" I cried, "No! I will not doubt; I cannot doubt." He then cleared the subject up so much to my mind that it was in fact impossible for me to doubt that the Spirit of God had taken possession of my soul.

In this state I was taught the doctrine of justification by faith, as a present experience. That doctrine had never taken any such possession of my mind, that I had ever viewed it distinctly as a fundamental doctrine of the Gospel. Indeed, I did not know at all what it meant in the proper sense. But I could now see and understand what was meant by the passage, "Being justified by faith, we have peace with God through our Lord Jesus Christ." I could see that the moment I believed, while up in the woods all sense of condemnation had entirely dropped out of my mind; and that from that moment I could not feel a sense of guilt or condemnation by any effort that I could make. My sense of guilt was gone; my sins were gone; and I do not think I felt any more sense of guilt than if I never had sinned.[8]

Though Finney is known as a preaching revivalist and reformer, there were occasions when the presence of God upon his life changed those around him without any words being spoken.

There was a cotton manufactory on the Oriskany creek, a little above Whitesboro, a place now called New York Mills. It was owned by a Mr. W——, unconverted, but a gentleman of high standing and good morals. My brother-in-law, Mr. G—— A——, was superintendent of the factory. I was invited to go, and went up one evening, and preached in the village schoolhouse, which was large, and was crowded with hearers. The word, I could see, took powerful effect among the people who were at work in the factory.

The next morning, after breakfast, I went into the factory, to look through it. As I went through, I observed there was a good deal of agitation among those who were busy at their looms, and their mules, and other implements of work. On passing through one of the apartments, where a great number of young women were attending to their weaving, I observed a couple of them eyeing me, and speaking very earnestly to each other; and I could see that they were a good deal agitated, although they laughed. I went slowly toward them. They saw me coming, and were evidently much excited. One of them was trying to mend a broken thread, and I observed that her hands trembled so that she could not mend it. I approached slowly, looking at the machinery, as I passed; but observed that this girl grew more and more agitated, and could not proceed with her work. When I came within eight or ten feet of her, I looked solemnly at her. She observed it, and was quite overcome, and sunk down, and burst into tears. The impression caught almost like powder, and in a few moments nearly all in the room were in tears. This feeling spread through the factory. Mr. W——, the owner of the establishment, was present, and seeing the state of things, he said to the superintendent, "Stop the mill, and let the people attend to religion; for it is more important that our souls should be saved than that this factory run." The gate was shut down, and the factory stopped; but where should we assemble? The superintendent suggested that the mule room was large; and, the mules being run up, we could assemble there. We did so, and a more powerful meeting I scarcely ever attended. It went on with great power. The revival went through the mill with astonishing power, and in the course of a few days nearly all in the mill were hopefully converted.[9]

Finney's mark on history is amazing. He demonstrates that life is never the same following an encounter with the face of God.

Just sitting in Finney's presence after this incident caused his boss to also flee to the woods in surrender to Christ. Finney would go on to set the nations ablaze with revival and evangelism. The very next day, he entered a church prayer meeting, and as he walked in, the power of God caused people to fall on the ground confessing their sins.

Finney also faced resistance. A man carried a pistol into one meeting, intending to kill him, before he was gripped with conviction and repented. A pastor tried to keep Finney out of one town by threatening to stop him with cannons. Another pastor who publicly denounced Finney in his church died immediately after speaking against him. In one city where Finney traveled, he met initial resistance, but when he began to preach, fear began to grip everyone and they fell to the ground in repentance. "If I had had a sword on each hand, I could not have cut them down as fast as they fell," he said. Many of them had to be carried out of the meeting, which lasted all night long. In another city, an entire tenth of the population was converted.

After a life of itinerant evangelism, Finney taught theology at Oberlin College. Overall, he is credited for winning more than half a million souls to God. He also renounced slavery and allowed women to speak in church in a day when such views were unpopular.[10]

Smith Wigglesworth

Smith Wigglesworth was an illiterate plumber who was incapable of speaking in front of a crowd. He preferred serving in the background while his wife did the preaching. But after he encountered the face of God, he was changed into a mighty healing revivalist.

> For four days I wanted nothing but God. But after that, I felt I should leave for my home, and I went to the Episcopal vicarage to say good-bye. I said to Mrs. Boddy, the vicar's wife: "I am going away, but I have not received the tongues yet." She answered, "It is not tongues you need, but the Baptism." "I have received the Baptism, Sister," I protested, "but I would like to have you lay hands on me before I leave." She laid her hands on me and then had to go out of the room. The fire fell. It was a wonderful time as I was there with God alone. He bathed me in power. I was conscious of the cleansing of the precious Blood, and I cried out: "Clean! Clean! Clean!" I was filled with the joy of the consciousness of the cleansing. I was given a vision in which I saw the Lord Jesus Christ. I beheld the empty Cross, and I saw Him exalted at the right hand of God the Father. I could speak no longer in English but I began to praise Him in other tongues as the Spirit of God gave me utterance. I knew then, although I might have received anointings previously, that now, at last I had received the real baptism in the Holy Spirit as they received on the day of Pentecost.[11]

After Mrs. Boddy had prayed for him, Wigglesworth telegraphed his wife, who, along with the rest of their Holiness people, didn't believe in a separate baptism of the Holy Spirit, nor in the gift of tongues. The telegraph, sent on Tuesday, October 28, 1907, read, "I have received the Baptism in the Holy Ghost and I have spoken in Tongues."[12]

Polly Wigglesworth responded to her husband:

> "I want you to understand that I am as much baptized as you are and I don't speak in tongues...I have been preaching for twenty years and you have sat beside me on the platform, but on Sunday you will preach yourself and I'll see what there is in it." Although fully involved in the work he used to struggle to speak publicly and left all the preaching to her. He had to win over his wife before he could win the approval of the rest of the folk at the mission.
>
> Polly had thrown down the gauntlet and the next Sunday she sat on a bench at the back of the hall. When it was the time for the message Smith walked the three steps up to the platform and as he did God gave him the passage from Isaiah 61:1–3 (KJV) *"The Spirit of the Lord God is upon me..."* and He was. Smith preached fluently under a heavy anointing and didn't break down and weep as he had done on previous occasions. Smith himself said, "Suddenly I felt that I had prophetic utterances which were flowing like a river by the power of the Holy Spirit."
>
> Polly couldn't believe what she was seeing and hearing. She shuffled up and down the bench and said in a whisper but still loud enough for those around her to hear, "That's

not my Smith, that's not my Smith…Amazing, amazing…what's happened to the man!"

He was indeed different. First the secretary of the
mission then his son George all wanted what he had and
the meeting ended in holy laughter with many in the congregation rolling around on the floor. This was just the
beginning and the years that followed saw their ministry
grow and develop.[13]

This is one of my favorite stories in all history. It illustrates
that there are different measures of the presence of God upon a life.
This account of Wigglesworth's life makes me hunger for more.

There were eleven leading Christians in prayer with our
Brother at a special afternoon meeting. Each had taken a
part. The Evangelist then began to pray for the Dominion, and as he continued, each, according to their measure
of spirituality, got out. The power of God filled the room
and they could not remain in an atmosphere supercharged
by the power of God.

The author on hearing of this from one who was present
registered a vow that if the opportunity came, he at any
rate would remain whoever else went out. During the stay
in the Sounds a special meeting was called to pray for the
other towns in New Zealand yet to be visited. A like position to the other meeting now arose. Here was the opportunity, the challenge, the contest was on. A number prayed.
Then the old saint began to lift up his voice, and strange as
it may seem, the exodus began. A Divine influence began

to fill the place. The room became holy. The power of God began to feel like a heavy weight. With set chin, and a definite decision not to budge, the only other one now left in the room hung on and hung on, until the pressure became too great, and he could stay no longer. With the flood gates of his soul pouring out a stream of tears, and with uncontrollable sobbing he had to get out or die; and a man who knew God as few do was left alone immersed in an atmosphere that few men could breathe in.[14]

Remember that this remarkable experience happened to a most unlikely vessel, and let it encourage you to qualify to receive more of God's Spirit because of your unrestrained hunger for Him.

After this, everything changed for Wigglesworth. He only had to walk past people, and they would come under the conviction of the Holy Spirit and turn to Jesus for salvation. Increasingly, miracles and healings occurred. The glory of God fell whenever he prayed or preached.

Blind eyes were opened, deaf ears were healed, cancers were cured, and the wheelchair-bound began to walk again. Besides all that, people were raised from the dead, fourteen of them over the course of the evangelist's ministry. In one famous account, he and a friend went to a hospital to pray for a sick woman. While they were praying, she died. Wigglesworth wouldn't accept that result. He pulled her body out of the bed and stood her against the wall, saying, "In the name of Jesus I rebuke this death." Her body began to tremble. He said, "In the name of Jesus, walk," and she did.[15]

This illiterate plumber traveled widely in Europe, Asia, New Zealand, and the United States. When crowds became too large for him to pray personally for everyone, he began to do what he called "wholesale healing," during which he would have everybody who needed healing lay hands on themselves while he prayed. Many people—sometimes hundreds of people—would be healed simultaneously.[16]

Wigglesworth's ministry was based on four principles: First, read the Word of God. Second, consume the Word of God until it consumes you. Third, believe the Word of God. Fourth, act on the Word of God.[17]

T. L. Osborn

T. L. Osborn had gone to India without any of the success he expected. He told his wife that if he could see Jesus, his life would be changed.

> The next morning at six o'clock, I was awakened by a vision of Jesus Christ as He came into our room. I looked upon Him. I saw Him like I see anyone. No tongue can tell of His splendor and beauty. No language can express the magnificence and power of His person. Of all I had heard and read about Him, the half had never been told me. His hands were beautiful; they seemed to vibrate with creative ability. His eyes were streams of love, pouring forth into my innermost being. When I came out of that room, I was a new man. Jesus had become the Master of my life. I knew the truth; He is alive; He is more than a

dead religion. My life was changed. I would never be the same. Old traditional values began to fade away, and I felt impressed daily by a new and increasing sense of reverence and serenity. Everything was different. I wanted to please Him. That is all that has mattered since that unforgettable morning.[18]

As a result of his face-to-face encounter, T. L. Osborn showed Jesus to the world. His accomplishment was the fulfillment to Acts 4:33. He writes, "Among the people of these many nations of the world, with great power [we] give witness of the resurrection of the Lord Jesus: and great grace is upon us all." He did what Jesus promised and did greater works than Jesus did. Here is a summary of accomplishments of his ministry in seventy nations of the world.

He states:

We saw deaf-mutes by the hundreds perfectly restored. We have seen great numbers of the blind instantly receive their sight as many as ninety cases in a single gospel crusade. We have seen the hopeless cripples restored—those in wheelchairs as long as forty-two years, arise and walk. Those on cots and stretchers have arisen and have been made whole. We have witnessed eardrums, lungs, kidneys, ribs and other parts of the body, which have been removed by operations, recreated and restored by God's creative power. We have seen incurables made well, cancers die and vanish, lepers cleansed, even the dead raised. In a single campaign which we have conducted, as many as 125 deaf-mutes, 90 totally blind, and hundreds of other equally miraculous deliverances have resulted. Happy and joyful confessions of Christ as Savior have numbered as many as 50,000 in one crusade, often many thousands in one night. What we have seen our Lord accomplish in the past is an example of what He yearns to do in every nation under Heaven.[19]

The apostle Paul

Paul hated Christians, and seemed to be an unlikely candidate for a God encounter. But God chose him, and he was changed. The following is the record of that encounter from *The Message* Bible.

All this time Saul was breathing down the necks of the Master's disciples, out for the kill. He went to the Chief Priest and got arrest warrants to take to the meeting places in Damascus so that if he found anyone there belonging to the Way, whether men or women, he could arrest them and bring them to Jerusalem.

He set off. When he got to the outskirts of Damascus, he was suddenly dazed by a blinding flash of light. As he fell to the ground, he heard a voice: "Saul, Saul, why are you out to get me?"

He said, "Who are you, Master?"

"I am Jesus, the One you're hunting down. I want you to get up and enter the city. In the city you'll be told what to do next."

His companions stood there dumbstruck—they could hear the sound, but couldn't see anyone—while Saul, picking himself up off the ground, found himself stone-blind. They had to take him by the hand and lead him into Damascus. He continued blind for three days. He ate nothing, drank nothing.

There was a disciple in Damascus by the name of Ananias. The Master spoke to him in a vision: "Ananias."

"Yes, Master?" he answered.

"Get up and go over to Straight Avenue. Ask at the house of Judas for a man from Tarsus. His name is Saul. He's there praying. He has just had a dream in which he saw a man named Ananias enter the house and lay hands on him so he could see again."

Ananias protested, "Master, you can't be serious. Everybody's talking about this man and the terrible things he's been doing, his reign of terror against your people in Jerusalem! And now he's shown up here with papers from the Chief Priest that give him license to do the same to us."

But the Master said, "Don't argue. Go! I have picked him as my personal representative to non-Jews and kings and Jews. And now I'm about to show him what he's in for—the hard suffering that goes with this job."

So Ananias went and found the house, placed his hands on blind Saul, and said, "Brother Saul, the Master sent me, the same Jesus you saw on your way here. He sent me so you could see again and be filled with the Holy Spirit." No sooner were the words out of his mouth than something like scales fell from Saul's eyes—he could see again! He got to his feet, was baptized, and sat down with them to a hearty meal.

Saul spent a few days getting acquainted with the Damascus disciples, but then went right to work, wasting no time, preaching in the meeting places that this Jesus was the Son of God. They were caught off guard by this and, not at all sure they could trust him, they kept saying, "Isn't this the man who wreaked havoc in Jerusalem among the believers? And didn't he come here to do the same thing—arrest us and drag us off to jail in Jerusalem for sentencing by the high priests?"

But their suspicions didn't slow Saul down for even a minute. His momentum was up now and he plowed straight into the opposition, disarming the Damascus Jews and trying to show them that this Jesus was the Messiah.

After this had gone on quite a long time, some Jews conspired to kill him, but Saul got wind of it. They were watching the city gates around the clock so they could kill him. Then one night the disciples engineered his escape by lowering him over the wall in a basket.

Back in Jerusalem he tried to join the disciples, but they were all afraid of him. They didn't trust him one bit. Then Barnabas took him under his wing. He introduced him to the apostles and stood up for him, told them how Saul had seen and spoken to the Master on the Damascus Road and how in Damascus itself he had laid his life on the line with his bold preaching in Jesus' name.

> After that he was accepted as one of them, going in and
> out of Jerusalem with no questions asked, uninhibited as
> he preached in the Master's name.
>
> —ACTS 9:1–28, THE MESSAGE

The effect of Paul's face-to-face encounter is so obvious it almost goes without saying. He turned the world upside down. The Lord transformed Paul and used his past training to make him the perfect interpreter of the old and new covenants. He guided the fledgling church through incredibly complex theological issues. Through teaching, courage, sacrificial love, and miraculous signs he birthed many of the churches from which worldwide revival would later spring. The Spirit so anointed him in thought and deed that his church "newsletters" were rightly recognized as God-breathed Scripture. Next to Jesus, he is considered by believers and unbelievers alike as one of the most influential men who ever lived.

Heidi Baker

Heidi and Rolland Baker are personal heroes, as they are for most everyone who knows them. Born into affluence, Heidi has spent her life with the poor. But it was the unusual encounter with God that enabled her to ignite the transformation of a nation through signs and wonders.

Although they had been laboring as missionaries in Mozambique for seventeen years, they had seen only marginal progress. They longed for more. In Heidi's words, "Rolland and

I so loved the manifest presence of God that we longed to be wherever He was pouring out His Spirit."[20]

They made several trips to Toronto to visit the Toronto Airport Christian Fellowship. That's where they were in January of 1998, when Randy Clark was preaching about the apostolic anointing. Suddenly:

> He pointed to me and said, "God is asking, 'Do you want Mozambique?'" I experienced the heavenly fire of God falling on me. I was so hot I literally thought I was going to burn up and die. I remember crying out, "Lord, I'm dying!" I heard the Lord clearly speak to my heart, "Good, I want you dead!" He wanted me completely emptied of self so He could pour even more of His Spirit into my life.
>
> For seven days I was unable to move. Rolland had to pick me up and carry me. I had to be carried to the washroom, to the hotel and back to the meeting. The weight of His glory was upon me. I felt so heavy I could not lift my head. Some passing by thought it was funny to see someone stuck to the floor for so long. If I were put in a chair, I would slide out onto the floor again. I was utterly and completely helpless. I was unable to speak for most of the seven days. This holy, fearful, awesome presence of God completely changed my life. I've never been so humbled, never felt so poor, so helpless, so vulnerable. I even needed help to drink water. There was nothing funny about it. It was a most holy time. I learned more in those seven days than in ten years of academic theological study.

The Lord spoke to me about relinquishing control to Him. He showed me the importance of the Body of Christ. It had taken us seventeen years to plant four churches, and two of them were pretty weak. As I lay there engulfed in His presence, he spoke to me about hundreds of churches being planted in Mozambique. I remember laughing hysterically, thinking I would have to live to be two hundred years old before that promise was fulfilled![21]

Heidi had been a type A person, driving to accomplish things in her own strength. She says that her mother had told her that even as a young child she used to line up all the little preschoolers and make them follow her. Now she was broken and humbled. She writes, "I thought I had been depending on Him to plant churches when in reality I depended a lot on my own abilities. Naturally things moved pitifully slowly....He showed me how much I needed Him and the Body of Christ."[22] Ephesians 4:1–6 took on new meaning:

> Therefore I, the prisoner of the Lord, implore you to walk in a manner worthy of the calling with which you have been called, with all humility and gentleness, with patience, showing tolerance for one another in love, being diligent to preserve the unity of the Spirit in the bond of peace.
>
> There is one body and one Spirit, just as also you were called in one hope of your calling; one Lord, one faith, one baptism, one God and Father of all who is over all and through all and in all.

After that transforming experience in Toronto, everything changed in the Bakers' ministry. They had been reduced to a place of utter dependence on Him. In the spirit of Ephesians 4:1–6, they began to release co-workers into the work as never before, imparting the anointing and delegating responsibilities. Even children were released to minister. As others were released, the ministry exploded.[23]

I have been to Mozambique with Rolland and Heidi Baker and have seen firsthand the amazing impact of their love for people. Of all the miracles I've seen through the years, one stands out from my recent visit. Heidi was praying for a man who was blind. In fact, all he had was the white of his eyes. It was as though there was a thick milky white film covering them. She prayed over him for about an hour. Nothing happened. She then told him to come back tomorrow and he would see. He did. And God healed him. He was actually the second blind person healed that day. Both of them, along with a great number of other new believers, were taken across the street to the ocean to be baptized.

The encounter that Heidi had with God has been imparted to their leadership core. And the same basic encounter that she had was released over their team. As a result of this outpouring on their leadership base of fourteen people, there have been approximately one million conversions to Christ. Over six thousand orphans are fed daily—sometimes even through the multiplying of food. Whereas it took them seventeen years to plant four churches before Heidi's encounter with God's face, they have planted over six thousand churches in the eight years since. As of the writing of this book, there have been over eighty people raised from the dead. The blind see, the deaf hear, and the lame walk with regularity. Entire Muslim villages come to Christ because of these miracles. This is one of the greatest missionary stories in all of history. And it continues to happen right now—all because of the quest for God's face.

Now What

It is impossible for me to read the stories of these men and women of God and remain the same. As a result the fire that burns in my soul gets hotter and brighter for more of God. Through their testimonies I know that such possibilities exist and the pursuit of them is worth any price. They inspire me to take risks for God and pursue Him even more. But most of all I learn to be grateful, but not satisfied.

I remember when I was a child and my parents would have guests come over to our house to visit. It was always exciting to be a part of the food and the fun. But it was painful to have to go to bed while they were still there, sitting in our living room, talking and having fun. The laughter that echoed back into my room was just torture. It was impossible for me to sleep in that atmosphere. Sometimes, when I couldn't take it any longer, I would sneak quietly into the hallway, just to listen. I didn't want to miss anything. If my parents caught me they usually sent me back to bed. But there were a few times when they thought my curiosity was humorous enough to let me come out to be with them just a little longer. The risk was worth it!

I'm in the hallway again. And the thought of missing something that could have been the experience of my generation is pure torture. I can't possibly sleep in this atmosphere, because if I do, I know I'll miss the reason for which I was born.[24]

CHAPTER 8

JOY: THE REWARD

The birth of Christ was proclaimed with this declaration: "I bring you good news of great joy!"[1] Apparently there is *normal* joy and then there is *great* joy. The coming of the Son of God to Earth was joyful news that would bring all who received Him into joy itself.

For reasons unknown to me, one of the greatest offenses in this present move of God is the manifestation of joy. Every season that brings new outpourings of the Holy Spirit (revival) interjects a new experience and manifestation that causes offense. It is necessary. Only when we are able to get past the fear of the criticism of others that such an experience brings are we poised to receive all that God has for us. The fear of man is the heart and soul of religion—form without power. And most of us are prone to try and bottle up what God is doing so we can analyze and control it to keep us comfortable. It is the way of death. And it must be defeated in us.

People seem to be good with the idea of joy as a theological value, but they disdain it as actual experience, especially as a corporate expression. It appears to be out of order. And it is. But whose order does joy actually violate?

DISORDERLY ORDER

I was present at the birth of all three of my children. It was wonderful, amazing—and very offensive. While the doctors would have said that everything was "decent and in order," it didn't look that way to me. Even though there was laughter and celebration, there was also a big mess with pain and tears. Those in charge didn't seem to be bothered by any of it. But to the uninitiated, it appeared chaotic. The nurses' and doctors' lack of panic helped to calm any misgivings I may have had about the situation.

> *Joy appears to be out of order. And it is. But whose order does joy actually violate?*

I wonder how often God has purposed to do something wonderful for His people, and then we get nervous and take over the controls because we don't feel comfortable with the situation. I've come to realize that He is not all that concerned about us feeling comfortable. That's why He gave us the Comforter—He planned to make us uncomfortable first.

The biggest offense in joy is laughter. The question comes often: Where is that in the Bible? It's not that complicated. Laughter is to salvation what tears are to repentance. We are not commanded to cry at an altar when we come to Christ. But it happens often, as it should. Our twisted set of values has distorted the nature of life with Christ. "In Your presence is fullness of joy; in Your right hand there are pleasures forever" (Psalm 16:11). Is not laughter at least a part of joy? Does not "fullness" mean that all the parts are joined together in the whole, whether it include laughter, smiling, inner happiness, or whatever else? While laughter should not be our only response to His presence, it is an acceptable and normal expression of being with God.

I have found that it usually takes greater faith to rejoice in His presence than it does to weep. To rejoice I have to believe that I am acceptable to God. I used to weep a lot with a sense of unworthiness. Hiding behind that was my inability to see that I was acceptable to God. But when people discover that not only are they acceptable to God, but also that He actually delights in them, it's time to rejoice! And if you want joy, rejoice.

THE EASE OF DIS-EASE

Much of the present Christian culture has unintentionally fostered ways of life and thought patterns that allow for people to be heavily burdened and discouraged as the norm. That habit often takes us into the stronghold of unbelief. In this mode we are much better at applauding tears over laughter, poverty over wealth, and the endurance of affliction over receiving quick answers and getting breakthroughs.

Our perspective is in need of change. An incorrect view of suffering has allowed the Trojan horse of disease to come in through the gates of the community of the redeemed. Misunderstanding this simple subject has invited the thief to come through the front door, often escorted by the teaching from our greatest pulpits.

The sufferings of Jesus were realized in the persecution He endured and in the burden He carried for people. He did not suffer with disease. That must be removed from our idea of Christian suffering. It is vain to carry something under the guise of the will of God when it is something that He purchased that He might destroy its power over us. An additional concept to remember is that He suffered that we *might not* have to suffer. For example, He bore stripes on His body applied by a Roman soldier so that they could become His payment for our healing.[2]

If this suffering of His was insufficient, then what did it accomplish? This error, if carried through, brings the whole issue of conversion and forgiveness of sins into question. It's true that the sufferings of Jesus are not yet complete,[3] but they have to do with our call to righteous living in an unrighteous world. This brings pressures upon our lives that range from the realm of persecution for living for Christ to the burdens we bear as intercessors before our heavenly Father where we plead the case of the lost.

There are few prophetic declarations that are more appropriate for this hour than this word from Hosea:

My people are destroyed for lack of knowledge.

—HOSEA 4:6

Ignorance that exalts itself with a false sense of accomplishment for meeting religious requirements is one of our greatest enemies. For ignorance creates tolerance. And what we tolerate dominates.

When we allow sickness, torment, and poverty to be thought of as the God-ordained tools He uses to make us more like Jesus, we have participated in a very shameful act. There is no doubt He can use them, as He is also known to be able to use the devil himself for His purposes. (He can win with a pair of twos.) But to think these things are released into our lives through His *design*, or that He approved such things, is to undermine the work at Calvary. To do so one must completely disregard the life of Christ and the purpose of the cross. None of us would say that He died for my sins but still intends that I should be bound by sin habits. Neither did He pay for my healing and deliverance so I could continue in torment and disease. His provision for such things is not figurative: it is actual.

Furthermore, it dishonors the Lord to disregard His work in order to justify our difficulty to believe for the impossible. It is time to own up to the nature of the gospel and preach it for what it is. It is the answer for every dilemma, conflict, and affliction on the planet. Declare it with boldness, and watch Him invade Earth once again.[4]

How Big Is Your Devil?

This false approach to the Christian life also tends to inflate the power of the devil in the minds of believers. In the wrong atmosphere, complaining and criticism masquerades as information needed for our prayer lives. This mind-set leads us away from the kingdom where there is righteousness, peace, and joy and takes us to a realm of heaviness that emphasizes the devil's strategies and accomplishments. We were not commanded to keep a record of the devil's accomplishments. We were commanded to keep the testimony of God's wonderful work on the earth,[5] making His works our delight and the object of our fascination and study.[6] We are commanded to "feed on His faithfulness" (Psalm 37:3, NKJV). The atmosphere established around us is determined by what treasure we keep (the treasure revealed in our conversations).

It is not healthy to have a big devil and a small (impractical) God. It's not that the devil has no power or should be ignored. The apostle Paul taught us against such ignorance.[7] We just can't afford to be impressed by the one who is restricted in power when we serve an all-powerful God. I try to live in such a way that nothing ever gets bigger than my awareness of God's presence. When I lose that perspective, I find that I need to repent, change my focus, and come into the awe of God again.

Allowing the facts of the devil's work to masquerade as truth undermines joy, the obvious trait of those who are in the kingdom of God. Truth becomes evident only in the mind of Christ, and the mind of Christ is given to joy. "At that very time He rejoiced greatly in the Holy Spirit" (Luke 10:21). Here the word *rejoiced* suggests *shouting and leaping*—not quite the picture of Jesus given to us in movies or sermons.

THE MOTIVATION OF JESUS

Jesus lived in perfect obedience, both in motive and in action. Everything that Jesus did He did as a man dependent on God. We also know that Jesus took delight in doing His Father's will. But it was the Father who brought another element into the equation: "Jesus, the author and perfecter of faith, who for the joy set before Him endured the cross" (Hebrews 12:2). The Father added a reward that was so significant that it would bring the Son of man through the greatest suffering ever known to a human being. And this One, who was to pay the ultimate price, would receive the ultimate reward—joy. Joy is the reward.

There is a price to pay for following Christ. And there is also a reward for following Christ. Emphasizing the price without the reward is morbid. Going through the pain of discipline for any reason must have an outcome that is worthy of the pain. When the Father wanted to give the best reward to His own Son, He chose to give Him joy. What will people do in heaven who do not like joy?

Jesus knew that such a reward was well worth the price. This is difficult to comprehend. But joy is such a priceless commodity in heaven that it also became the reward for the believer. "Well done, good and faithful slave. . . . *Enter into the joy of your master*" (Matthew 25:21, emphasis added). The implication is not only that joy is the reward but also that we are to enter into our Father's personal joy. "He who sits in the heavens laughs" (Psalm 2:4). It is the very nature of God that we get to enjoy and celebrate for eternity. And part of that nature is seen in joy. Think of it as a mansion you have inherited. Your great privilege is to *enter* each room of that place with wonder and delight. While it's an honor just to be there, the shocking reality is that it is your inheritance. The whole unending realm of the Father's joy is your personal possession, and it's yours to explore for eternity. And for you, eternity started the moment you were born again.

> *Our joy is a direct result of being before the face of God. A countenance filled with joy is the reflection of the Father's delight in us.*

There are some who think it is carnal to do things to get a reward. Jesus's example should dispel such a notion. Rewards are a part of heaven's economy and are legitimate motivators. In fact, those who lose sight of their reward have not kept a healthy view of eternity. And we don't do well without eternity in mind.

THE JOY OF HIS FACE

Joy is an important part of the Father's nature. We experience His joy, and now we inherit His joy as our own. "Righteousness and justice are the foundation of Your throne; lovingkindness and truth go before You. How blessed are the people who *know the joyful sound*! O LORD, *they walk in the light of Your countenance.* In Your name they rejoice all the day, and by Your righteousness they are exalted" (Psalm 89:14–16, emphasis added).

Our joy is a direct result of being before the face of God. A countenance filled with joy is the reflection of the Father's delight in us. Those who live before the face of God know the sound of joy, for the sound of joy is the actual sound of heaven. There is no darkness in heaven, not even a shadow, because the light of His face is everywhere. In the same way, there is no discouragement or depression in heaven, because the sound of joy radiates from the face of God. Praying for the kingdom of God to come now "on earth as it is in heaven" (Matthew 6:10) is in essence a prayer for the atmosphere of heaven to permeate Earth—the atmosphere of joy.

JOYFUL MINDEDNESS

It is said that the mind of a child is trained in joy at an early age. It's as though boundaries are established much like a surveyor would go out onto a piece of property and drive stakes into the ground to mark the property lines. So children's capacity for joy and wholeness is set by their relationship with loving adults who are delighted in them. There is a part of the brain that some call the joy center. This area is activated through the joyful countenance of the parents as they look into the child's eyes. This affirming experience is their actual training for joy.

The book *Living From the Heart Jesus Gave You* states:

> In a child's first two years, the desire to experience joy in loving relationships is the most powerful force in life. In fact, some neurologists now say that the basic human need is to be the "sparkle in someone's eye." When you catch a glimpse of a child's face as she runs toward an awaiting parent with arms outstretched in unrestrained joy, you can witness firsthand that incredible power that comes from "being the sparkle in someone's eye." When this joy is the strongest force in a child's world, life makes sense, because children look forward to moments when they can re-connect to joy—by being with their beloved. Wonderfully enough, that innocent, pure desire that begins in childhood continues throughout life. Life makes sense and is empowered by joy when people are in relationship with those who love them and are sincerely "glad to be with them."[8]

This reveals why so many struggle with the subject of joy in the church. And more importantly, it shows why most have so little joy in their personal lives. They've not seen the favor and approval from their heavenly Father. The church is crippled in most of its Christian life because people view God as the One who longs to punish instead of save, the One who reminds them of sin instead of forgiving.

Jesus taught His disciples to seek the face of His Father. Those who do so get the affirming realization that we are the "sparkle in His eyes." From this place of intimacy with God we find answers and solutions. Concerning this, Jesus said, "Until now you have asked for nothing in My name; ask and you will receive, so *that your joy may be made full*" (John 16:24, emphasis added). Once again we see that joy is the expected result of a right relationship with God. It is normal. Everything below that is not. Some teach of the balanced Christian life as though we needed equal measures of joy and depression. Foolishness! The kingdom is one of joy. And I don't ever have to leave.

JOY BRINGS STRENGTH

For me the most surprising place to find one of the greatest revelations of joy is in the Old Testament. Thankfully, God allowed Israel to taste of the coming reality that would be had by all who were covered in the redemptive work of Christ. Furthermore, it came when the children of Israel had been standing from early morning until the evening listening to the priests read from the book of Law. Many of them were hearing the Law of God for the first time. When the people didn't understand what was read, priests would run out among the people giving explanation. They saw that God's standard of requirement for their lives was extremely high. They also saw that they had miserably failed God in what He required. This was a shocking moment. And they responded in the most natural way imaginable: with tears.

> Then Nehemiah, who was the governor, and Ezra the priest and scribe, and the Levites who taught the people said to all the people, "*This day is holy to the Lord your God; do not mourn or weep.*" For all the people were weeping when they heard the words of the law. Then he said to them, "Go, eat of the fat, drink of the sweet, and send portions to him who has nothing prepared; for this day is holy to our Lord. Do not be grieved, for *the joy of the Lord is your strength.*" So the Levites calmed all the people, saying, "Be still, for the day is holy; do not be grieved."
>
> —NEHEMIAH 8:9–11, EMPHASIS ADDED

Grieving and weeping over sin is thought to be very consistent with the subject of holiness. In our world, tears are almost synonymous with repentance. Yet not this time. In this context it was a violation. In my background it seems quite strange that there are times when the holiness of God is actually violated by tears. But it's true. There was much mourning and weeping because they saw that they had not even come close to God's purposes for their lives. That could only come about with an overwhelming conviction of the Holy Spirit that would give them the chance to see their hearts as He did. In all honesty, this is the kind of moment that many of us preachers look for—the people are aware of their need for God, aware of their need for forgiveness, and are ready to make a change. It's not out of cruelty. It is because we look for moments when people are ready to make permanent changes in their lives. And such brokenness is the climate of the heart that makes change possible. Yet the Spirit of God had another tool He purposed to use to bring about His intended transformation. It is the power of celebration—the power of joy.

The priests saw their tears and realized that this was in violation of what God was doing. Their responsibility was now to run out among the people and tell them to stop weeping! They were not only to stop weeping; they were to take it a step further into rejoicing and celebrating. The reason? They *understood* the law. Understanding what God was saying to them was to become the point of their joy, and thus the birth of their joy.

If ever there were a moment in the Old Testament that gave a sneak peak of New Testament life, it was this one. It violates all of our understanding of the severity of the Law and even violates our understanding of how God moves in revivals. For this reason many have missed the much-needed revelation of joy through grace that came forth in this present move of God. It is legitimate. It started with joy.

CHAPTER 9

REFLECTION OF THE FACE OF GOD

rue believers are being positioned to display the wonders of the almighty God to the world around us. The Bible actually calls us a new creation,[1] a new race of people that had never existed before.[2] Many of the prophecies that Jesus made concerning His church have never been fulfilled. The "greater works" of John 14:12 are yet to come upon an entire generation. But this is the hour all the prophets spoke of. Kings and prophets longed to see what we have seen. It is important that we say yes to all that has been provided for us through the blood of Jesus. It is time for the people of God to rise as one and display the power and glory of God.

Jesus once told a crowd of people, "If I do not do the works of My Father, do not believe Me" (John 10:37). Angels, the prophets, nature, and Scripture all testified about who Jesus was. Yet He was willing to hang the credibility of all those witnesses on one thing—the works of the Father. Without question, the works of the Father that Jesus is referring to are the miracles recorded throughout the Gospel of John.[3] If Jesus didn't do miracles, people were not required to believe. I look for the day when the church, His body, makes the same statement to the world around us: if we don't do the works of our Father, do not believe us.

PERFECT THEOLOGY

Jesus Christ is perfect theology. For anyone who wants to know the will of God, look at Jesus. He is the will of God. Some pray, "If it be Thy will," as though God's will is unclear. You would have to ignore the life of Christ to come to such a conclusion.

> *If we don't do the works of our Father, do not believe us.*

How many people came to Jesus for healing and left sick? None. How many came to Him for deliverance and left His presence still under torment? None. How many life-threatening storms did Jesus bless? None. How many times did Jesus withhold a miracle because the person who came to Him had too little faith? Never. He often addressed their small faith or unbelief, but He always left them with a miracle as a way to greater faith. Jesus Christ, the Son of God, perfectly illustrates the will of God the Father. To think otherwise is to put the Father and the Son at odds. And a house divided will fall.

Why did Jesus raise the dead? Because not everyone dies in God's timing. We cannot have the Father choosing to do one thing and Jesus contradicting it with a miracle. Not everything that happens is God's will. God gets blamed for so much in the name of His sovereignty. We have concealed our irresponsibility regarding the commission that Jesus gave us under the veil of God's sovereignty for long enough. Yes, God can use tragedy for His glory. But God's ability to rule over bad circumstances was never meant to be the evidence that those circumstances were His will. Instead it was to display that no matter what happens, He is in charge and will rework things to our advantage and to His glory. Our theology is not to be built on what God hasn't done. It is defined by what He does and is doing. The will of God is perfectly seen in the person of Jesus Christ. No one who ever came to Him was turned away.

The Bible celebrates the man healed by the pool of Bethesda.[4] If that were done today, the Christian periodicals would interview the people by the pool who were not healed. Theologians would then use the absence of a miracle for the others as a proof text, saying, "It's not always God's will to heal." In the absence of experience, bad theology is formed.

RE-PRESENTING JESUS

Everyone who confesses to know Jesus Christ in a personal relationship is assigned the privilege of re-presenting Him. "As the Father has sent Me, I also send you" (John 20:21). The mandate is clear and strong and there are no options. Discovering who He is and what He is like is the great journey for the believer. It is an eternal quest: one that we will delight in forever. But in our discovery is the responsibility to make Him known. Do we do so by preaching the Word? Yes. But He is also to become manifest through our lives. We are to become a portrait of God. This is part of what being the body of Christ means.

We become like that which we worship. Seeing Him changes us. Worship increases our capacity to see. But if we view God through an incomplete Old Testament lens, then we are likely to try to carry a message of wrath and anger, thinking we are honoring God. It's not that God cannot show anger. The whole point is that He wants to show mercy, and He looks for those who will intercede on behalf of those who have no hope. He is the One who said that mercy is victorious over judgment. An incomplete revelation from the old covenant cannot produce fruit of the new. Those who don't see Him through the New Testament revelation in Scripture try to re-create who He is through human reasoning. It is usually a distorted view of an angry God. But sometimes it's the other extreme where they preach about a God that ignores sin. Neither is correct, and both are products of the minds of those who cannot see.

He is perfect in *love, power, character,* and *wisdom.* These are the expressions of His nature that must be seen all at once—this time, in and through us.

LOVE

It is an honor to love, for God loved us first.[5] We only give away what we've received. God set the standard for giving love that demands nothing in return. He also set the standard for love that is sacrificial. "For God so loved the world, that He gave..." (John 3:16). It is our privilege to give time, money, attention, friendship, and so on. Sacrificial giving is sacrificial living. While we can give without loving, we can't love without giving. By nature love does not require anything in return, or it is not love. The real test of love is when we are able to love the unlovely, who are unable to give in return.

"*As the Father has sent Me, I also send you" (John 20:21). The mandate is clear and strong and there are no options.*

Many of us grew up thinking that the way we reach out to our community is to pray hard that people would attend church meetings in hopes of them being converted. It's hard for us to be effective in demonstrating the love of God if people are required to come to us. It is in *going* that we are most likely to give authentically.

The story of the good Samaritan stands out as a good example of love.[6] He adopted the problems of the injured stranger as his own. When he couldn't stick around to help the man firsthand, he hired someone to do what he was unable to do. It is an amazing story of loving a total stranger.

I have heard teaching on the subject of giving to the poor and needy that emphasizes our stewardship instead of compassion. It basically means that you don't want to give to someone who will not use what was given properly. My opinion is that there is too much concern about giving something to someone who might misuse what is given. That didn't stop God. While we do have a responsibility for good management of what God has given us, we are not responsible for what another person does with what we've given them. We are responsible to love, and love requires giving. Even if a person misuses the money or gift I gave them, the message of love has been demonstrated. Giving His love away is the goal.

People who get breakthroughs in the miracle realm face a temptation: it's easy to pursue miracles for miracles' sake. But the greater ambition ought to be that in all we do we display the love of God.

POWER

The tendency to embrace the concept of God being an angry Father is done in equal proportion to a person's inability to demonstrate His power. There is a connection between our belief system and what actually flows through us. If we don't see Jesus's life as ultimate illustration of the will of God, we will continually undermine our ability to display it.

Powerlessness is such an aberration that we are either compelled to seek for a fresh baptism in the Spirit until the power that was promised becomes manifested through us, or we create doctrinal reasons to comfort ourselves in powerlessness. I don't want comfort. I want power. It is never OK to live short of the miraculous. I am indebted to Him in this matter: He gave the example, sent the wonderful Holy Spirit, and gave us His Word in our commission. What else must He do? We owe Him miracles as a testimony that He is alive and that His face is turned toward us. The Spirit of the resurrected Christ, that same Spirit that anointed Jesus for ministry, lives within us. The Gospel makes sufficient provision for this issue to be settled for anyone who seeks His face with reckless abandon.

I've heard people say that if they had to choose between purity and power, they'd choose purity. That sounds good, but it's an illegal choice. The two must not be separated. They are two sides of the same coin, and they must remain intact. I have told our church family, "I'm not impressed with anyone's life that does not have character. But I'm not happy with that life until there is power."

CHARACTER

Christlike character is not merely being victorious over sin issues. It is the realized effect of the life of faith, which is righteousness,

peace, and joy, which is, as I have already made clear, Paul's definition of the kingdom.[7] These three things demonstrate the character of Christ in the life of a believer.

Living *righteously* means that I live completely for God, with
no attachments to ungodly things. Living for God means I reject
the inferior things that give temporary satisfaction because only
the kingdom of God satisfies. Righteousness has been reduced to
morality for some. Morality is essential, but it is the bottom rung
of the ladder. It's the first step. But true righteousness is demonstrated in Christlike indignation toward injustice. It seeks to vin-
dicate mistreatment of the poor, the widow, and the unborn. It
also stirs our hearts toward those who are bound by disease, for it
was the sun of *righteousness* that rose with healing in His wings.[8]
Healing is an expression of His righteousness on our behalf.

It saddens me to see Christians who will not associate with
unbelievers because they want to be separate from the world,
yet their lifestyles are the same as unbelievers. The early church
associated with unbelievers but didn't live like them. That day is
returning as the issue of character is being addressed once again,
this time rightly partnered with power.

Like peace and joy, righteousness is a gift. "Those who receive
the abundance of grace and of the gift of righteousness will reign
in life through the One, Jesus Christ" (Romans 5:17). The word
reign in this verse means "to be king." The imagery is strong.
Righteousness enables a person to exercise dominion over their
life and not live as a victim. Abraham's nephew, Lot, fell short
of this reality when the Scriptures say that he was "oppressed

by the sensual conduct of unprincipled men" (2 Peter 2:7). The conduct of others affected and oppressed him. Life in God has been designed in such a way that righteousness in our lives actually affects the people around us, much the same way as a king's reign affects everyone under his influence. This is a central theme in the subject of city transformation.

Peace is more than the absence of noise, conflict, and war. It is the presence of the One who exercises military authority over everything that is in conflict with His dominion. As we enjoy His order and calm, the powers of darkness are destroyed by His overwhelming magnificence. It is a life of *rest* for us but a life of *terror* for the powers of darkness. For this reason the Bible declares, "The God of peace will soon crush Satan under your feet" (Romans 16:20). As His peace comes upon us, our enemies are destroyed. When anxiety and fear approach, we must get back to our place of peace. It is our rightful inheritance in Christ and is the place from which we live. This attribute of heaven is the evidence of a victory that has already been won. It is this characteristic that so frustrates the devil. Our not being terrified by him because of our abiding peace actually terrifies the enemy of our soul.

Joy belongs to the believer. As I said in the previous chapter, joy is to salvation what tears are to repentance. It is one of the most essential expressions of abiding faith. Being stern and harsh is overrated. Any unbeliever can do that. Jesus was only this way toward those who rejected Him but should have known better. They called Him a drunk and glutton simply because drunks and gluttons experienced His love and acceptance. Faith believes I am accepted by God, and there is no power or authority that can take that away.

If you lack joy, there is one way you can engage in the process of gaining ever-increasing joy: learn to rejoice. A choice to rejoice cannot depend on circumstances, because it operates from the heart of faith. It lives regardless of what has happened, embracing the realities of His world that can only be accessed by trust in God and His Word. Rejoicing releases joy.

But perhaps the greatest secret regarding joy is in discovering God's joy over us. The Bible tells us, "The joy of the LORD is your strength" (Nehemiah 8:10). God has joy. And it's His joy over us that makes us strong! That truth sets us free unlike anything else. Rejoice, for He is delighted in you!

WISDOM[9]

Jesus is called *the desire of the nations.*[10] To make us successful in the commission to disciple nations He chose to live inside of us. This gives us the potential of appealing to the world around us. That is far from the present experience of most of us. While sinners loved to be with Jesus, they seldom like to be with us. It is up to us to find out why and fix it. Part of the reason is because we tend to be very impractical, answering questions that few people are asking, bringing direction that no one is looking for.

Yet it is God's time for His people to become highly esteemed by unbelievers again (we prefer to call them, "pre-believers"). Jesus has all the answers to all the world's problems. We have legal access to the mysteries of the kingdom. His world is the answer for this one. No matter the problem, whether it is medical, political, or as simple as a traffic-flow problem in our neighborhood or a conflict on the local school board, Jesus has the answers. Not only that, but He also desires to reveal them to us and through us. His method of choice is to use His children, the descendants of the Creator, to represent Him in such matters.

It's hard for us to bring solutions for this world's dilemmas when our hope (end-time theology) is eagerly anticipating the destruction of the planet. Both Jesus and the apostle Paul said we inherit this world.[11] Our correct stewardship should start now. To ignore this part of the commission because of the conviction that the world cannot be made perfect before Jesus's return is very similar to ignoring the poor because Jesus said they'd always be with us. It is irresponsible stewardship of our commission and anointing.

Wisdom is the creative expression of God.[12] It was a part of the creative force used in making the "all" that is. It is celebratory in nature, with a special delight in humanity.

Besides Jesus, Solomon is the one known most for extraordinary wisdom. In fact, Solomon's wisdom was the high watermark in Israel's history. With it he silenced the queen of Sheba when she came to sit at his feet and learn. He answered many questions about life that were puzzling to her. But when God chose to list the things that impressed her, He recorded a list that would normally be boring, that is, outside of wisdom. The Scriptures list them this way: *the house that he built, the food on his table, the seating of his servants, the service of his waiters and their apparel, his cupbearers, and his entryway by which he went up to the house of the Lord.*[13] These are all everyday things. Only the creative expression of God could arrest the heart of a queen with the ordinary. She had already seen wealth and treasures. She had been exposed to great talent and even craftsmanship. But she was now looking at mundane things that had taken on meaning through the creative expression of God through a man. And it made her speechless.

It's time for the world to become speechless again as they become aware of our approach to the simplicities of life—this time with divine wisdom.

THE RENEWED MIND

You know your mind is renewed when the impossible looks logical. The most consistent way to display the kingdom of God is through the renewed mind. It is much more than thinking right thoughts. It is how we think—from what perspective. Done correctly, we are to "reason" from heaven toward Earth.

Four *cornerstones of thought* have changed how we do life. They must become more than doctrines that we agree with. They must become perspectives that change how we approach life— attitudes that define the culture we have chosen to live in.

God is good. I often open our meetings on Sunday with this announcement: "God is in a good mood." It shocks people. As simple as it is, it is not really believed by very many people.

But God is really secure in His sovereignty, and He rejoices in the bride of His Son. God thinks the price paid is worth what they're getting. The ones with the angry messages from our pulpits just need to meet the Father. He is really good, all the time. He's better than we think, so let's change the way we think.

"Nothing is impossible" has become a slogan that defines our approach to life. As believers we are assigned to invade what has previously been called impossible. Some Christians shy away from the pursuit of miracles because they consider them impossible. The saddest part of their story is that they think the rest of the Christian life is possible. Not so! The whole thing is impossible to the natural mind. Only God can say from experience, "Nothing is impossible." But to give us access to a realm that only He enjoys, He added, "All things are possible for him who believes" (Mark 9:23).

> *The most consistent way to display the kingdom of God is through the renewed mind.*

We fight from the victory of Christ. We do not do warfare in order to win. Rather it is to enforce the victory that Jesus has already won on our behalf. We war from His victory toward a given situation. That changes our perspective, which is half the battle. For the believer, most closed heavens are between the ears. When we believe things are dark and feed our soul on that reality, we have a big battle to fight. Through intimidation the enemy has succeeded in putting us into a defensive posture. It's the wrong position—we are on offense and we have the ball. We've had it ever since Jesus commanded us to "*go* into all the world" (Mark 16:15, emphasis added).

I am significant. It is easier to say that *we* are significant, instead of saying *I am significant.* Yet it is the discovery of this truth that liberates us into true humility. Anyone who speaks of his or her own significance, but goes into pride, never really got this important revelation. There is a humility that comes from seeing our past. But the greater measure of humility comes from seeing our future. What is before us is impossible without God's favor, strength, and guidance. Dependency on Him is the result of the discovery of personal significance.

GOD'S ULTIMATE PLAN

God has turned our hearts once again to seek His face. Prayer movements are springing up in most every stream of the body of Christ. What Lou Engle has done with The Call[14] is literally shaping the course of history as an entire generation is being summoned by God to change a nation through prayer and intercession. In light of this shift in the Spirit, we too must embrace the call to pray. But as we do, let's learn to pray as Jesus did.

For the believer, most closed heavens are between the ears.

There is no record of Jesus asking His Father to heal someone, nor is there record of Him crying for the Father's deliverance in a life-threatening storm. Instead He had gained a place of authority in prayer so that He could simply bring the command and watch the will of His Father being done.

It's time to use a good part of our prayer time to actually seek His face. The result will be clearly seen, for when we speak, things will happen—and when we touch people in ministry, we will bring them into an encounter with God that changes everything.

CHAPTER 10

A PEOPLE OF HIS GLORY

*J*esus Christ was entirely God. He was not a created being. Yet He became a man and lived entirely within man's limitations. His ability to demonstrate power, walk on water, and carry out countless other divine manifestations was completely due to the fact that He was without sin and was totally yielded to the Holy Spirit. He became the model for everyone who would experience the cleansing of sin by the blood of Jesus.

The forgiveness that God gives puts every believer in a place without sin. The only question that remains is how empowered by the Holy Spirit we are willing to be.

EXPERIENCES FOR SONS AND DAUGHTERS

Most all of the experiences of Jesus recorded in Scripture were prophetic examples of the realms in God that are made available to the believer. The Mount of Transfiguration raised the bar significantly on potential human experience. The goal should never be to talk with Moses and Elijah, and anyone who has that as a focus would concern me. The overwhelming lesson in this story is that Jesus Christ, the *Son of man*, had the glory of God upon Him. Jesus's face shone with God's glory, similar to Moses's after he came down from the mountain.[1] But Jesus's clothing also radiated the glory of God, as if to say this was a new era as compared to Moses's day. In this era the boundaries had changed—a veil could not be used to cover Jesus's face as it shone with glory, as the veil itself would also soon radiate with the same glory. We influence and impart what God has given us to change the nature of whatever we touch. Remember that touching the edge of Jesus's garment healed a woman. In this kingdom, things are different.

Only Peter, James, and John were privileged to be a part of this event. It was so extreme that Jesus warned them not to tell anyone about what they had seen until after His Resurrection. His death would satisfy the requirements of both the Law (Moses) and the prophets (Elijah). Certain things have no place in our hearts until we know of the Resurrection through our own conversion experience. Through the Spirit of the resurrected Christ living in us we are designed to carry the same glory. But we still must go up the mountain[2]—to the place where we meet with God face to face.

Preceding this experience Jesus made the declaration, "There are some standing here who will not taste death till they see the kingdom of God present with power" (Mark 9:1, NKJV). I do not think He was referring to the Mount of Transfiguration experience, which was only six days later. He was referring to the baptism in the Holy Spirit that would become available after His death and resurrection. That is "the kingdom of God present with power."

WHY NOT NOW?

It is theological irresponsibility to have the great promises of Scripture and put them off into a period of time for which we have no responsibility. It has become way too easy to place everything that's good into the Millennium and keep the trials and dark seasons for this era. My greatest difficulty with that line of thinking is that it requires no faith to achieve it, and that seems to be inconsistent with the rest of God's dealings with humanity. It also places an unhealthy emphasis on future generations to the point where we lose our sense of purpose, call, and destiny. While I live to leave a legacy, each generation has been given enough favor from the Lord to consider themselves capable of being the "final" generation that lives in the glory of God, for the glory of God.

One of my favorite declarations in Scripture is found in Isaiah 60:1, "Arise, shine; for your light has come!" People stumble over determining the audience to which this command is addressed. Some would put this off into God's future dealings with Israel, which I believe to be a great mistake. While God's great plan is being worked out in His people Israel, the command is brought to *all who have received* His light. What is that light, and to whom has this light come?

Jesus Christ is the light of the world. He enlightens every person that comes into this world. "In Him was life, and the life was the Light of men.... There was the true Light which, coming into the world, enlightens every man" (John 1:4, 9).

When Isaiah made the declaration to *arise* and *shine*, it was a command reserved for those who received the light that Jesus brought into the world. He is that light. And those who received His light unto salvation are required to *arise*. It is a command. Many wait for something else to happen to them. But He says, "Get up, now! And while you're getting up, shine!"

This amazing declaration began to unfold in Jesus's day, because the second part of the declaration was fulfilled—He, the light, *had* come. But before Jesus left, He told His disciples that they were the light of the world. That statement is often considered figurative language, which is disastrous when God is speaking literally. The church *is* the light of the world.

When the light of God touches you, you become light. In whatever fashion God touches our lives we become a manifestation of that very reality. It's one of the great mysteries in the gospel, testifying of its ability to completely transform the nature of everything it touches. This issue of *becoming light* is not an isolated illustration, which we will see. It is the power of the gospel that completely transforms the nature of whatever it touches.

Jesus is our righteousness. But when we are touched by His righteousness, we not only became righteous, but we also became *the righteousness of God*.[3] Consider this extreme effect of the gospel. We don't just carry this grace from God. We become a manifestation of that grace. When we think only in figurative and symbolic language we undermine the power of God's intent. With such extraordinary promises we must not be a people restricted by the boundaries set by a prior generation. We must instead build upon their experience and go where they didn't have time to go.

> *We actually broker God's forgiveness.*

God takes this to another extreme in the subject of forgiveness. When you are forgiven, you become a forgiver. Jesus pressed way past my comfort zone by saying, "If you forgive the sins of any, their sins have been forgiven them; if you retain the sins of any, they have been retained" (John 20:23). We actually broker God's forgiveness. At minimum God is saying that when we forgive people, God moves upon them with His forgiveness. Again, our nature has been changed by the way in which God touched us.

COVENANTS IN CONFLICT

Under the Old Testament, if you touch a leper, you become unclean. The primary message of that covenant was to reveal the power of sin. But the Law of God was not the answer to the problem of sin. It was incapable of being the solution. It was the tutor that was intended to lead people to Christ. As people discovered they could not become righteous on their own, the Law created such a tension in people's lives that it successfully prepared Israel for the Savior. And so, touching the leper made you unclean.

But in the New Testament we touch the leper and the leper becomes clean. That's because the primary message of this covenant is the power of God's love to make us whole. When we demonstrate authentic love, He backs it up with kingdom power. The one who is cleansed by the blood of Jesus is now able to cleanse; this was in the commission Jesus gave to His disciples: "Cleanse the lepers" (Matthew 10:8).

By the hundreds of millions, people recognize the power of sin. They live under the realization that they cannot change their nature. And so they spend their lives changing the color of their hair, taking off pounds, and learning new skills to somehow quench that internal desire for personal transformation. Some rebel against that desire and surrender to the inevitable by giving themselves over to a sin nature they cannot control. The results are in our newspaper headlines daily.

But the power of sin is old news! The news needed in this day is that the power of the authentic love of God transforms everything it touches. Those changed by His love are true lovers, and those who don't love others have no evidence of ever having experienced God's love.[4] As we face Him, our nature is changed into the nature of the One who touched us, and we release the power of His love to those around us.

We Must Shine

One of the issues that must be settled in the minds of believers if we are going to obey God's command to arise and shine is the issue of being glorious. For many Christians, the idea of being glorious sounds prideful or ridiculous. But there is a glory that exists in humanity simply because we were made in His image. There is a glory in animals, the sun, the stars, and all other created things.[5] He made it this way.

To downplay our role in these last days and to *play small* in life restricts the measure of glory we possess and are able to give to God. Our capacity to give glory ends up being reduced by our unbelief in our significance. Our significance is not based on anything in and of us. It is entirely based on the One who calls us to Himself.

Solomon seemed to know this, saying, "Let another praise you, and not your own mouth; a stranger, and not your own lips" (Proverbs 27:2). God warns against boasting in ourselves, but He adds that we are to allow others to do it to us. Honor is a kingdom value. If we don't know how to receive it correctly, we will have no crown to throw at His feet. Our war against pride is misguided when it is inconsistent with God's Word. False humility is the most dangerous form of pride as it is often mistaken for a virtue.

When people give me honor, I thank them for their thoughtfulness. But I refuse to respond with the nauseating religious jargon, "It wasn't me; it was Jesus." Rather, when I get alone with God, I bring the honor given to me and give it to Him, saying,

"Look what someone gave to me. I believe this belongs to You." There's no question in my mind about who really deserves it.

It's just fascinating to me that He enjoys having us be *in the line of fire* when glory and honor are being released. They affirm our eternal significance and destiny. And if we make the mistake of taking that honor to ourselves, then we have already received our reward in this life. The eternal aspect has been removed. That which is invested into eternity pays eternal dividends. Is it possible that the scriptural standard of going from *glory to glory* also carries with it the principle of going from living in the glory of man to living in the glory of God?

Jesus added to this command, saying, "Let your light shine before men in such a way that they may see your good works, and glorify your Father who is in heaven" (Matthew 5:16). There is a way in which we can shine that causes others to worship God and give Him glory. It was in this context that Jesus taught us that our lights were not to be hidden but put in the open for others to see. Others are attracted to God by our shining.

How to Shine

To learn how to shine in response to God's command in Isaiah 60 we must learn how God shines. We represent Him. Here is the blessing that Aaron and his sons were to release over the children of Israel.

The LORD bless you, and keep you;

The LORD make His face shine on you,

And be gracious to you;

The LORD lift up His countenance on you,

And give you peace.

—NUMBERS 6:24–26

When God shows His favor to people He is giving us a model to follow. He is teaching us how to shine. Showing favor to others is one way to follow His example. Being accepted by God enables us to accept others, once again demonstrating that we become a manifestation of the nature of God's touch in our lives. In this light Paul makes an interesting statement to the church at Ephesus:

Let no unwholesome word proceed from your mouth, but only such a word as is good for edification according to the need of the moment, so that *it will give grace* to those who hear.

—EPHESIANS 4:29, EMPHASIS ADDED

As we have seen, God's face shines on us when He releases His favor and blessing in our lives. We have been given the power to release life and death through our speech.[6] In this place of responsibility we are able to speak words that encourage according to the needs a person has at the moment. But the part of the verse that amazes me the most is that we are able to *give grace to those who hear.* Grace is divine favor. In a sense we broker God's favor. It is as though He is saying, *To whomever you show favor, I will show favor.* Every time you bring encouragement to someone, you release divine favor. They are marked for God's attention because of your words. That is shining!

Several years ago one of our young men was in court for a crime he committed before his conversion. I testified on his behalf. He had already spent time in prison for a previous crime and could be sent back for a long time. His life had been transformed by Christ, which was publicly noted by both the judge and the prosecuting attorney. But the prosecutor still asked that he be sent to jail.

They found him guilty and sent him to a conservation camp for six months. I was hoping they'd let him go without any prison time, because for the first time in his life he had a good job and was a contributor to society. I wrote a letter to the judge stating that while I was hoping my friend wouldn't have any more time in jail, I thanked him for taking a stand for justice, and I told him that we appreciated his work for our community. I also thanked him for the mercy he showed in such a short sentence. He wrote back with thanks, saying, "We don't receive letters like this." Honor was due, and it was a privilege to give it. And it takes so little time to give it away; it's one of the ways we shine.

We are witnessing the power of honor in society. We can give it even before a person is born again. City life is changing through this simple tool. Whether it's the business person who invests hard-earned dollars into our city or the waitress who works long hours to take care of her child at home, they are all hungry for significance. And that need is met through honor.

GIVING AWAY THE FARM

It's commonly said, "You can't out-give God." And it's true. He makes sure that we receive mostly according to what we've given away. But it's not simply because God gives back to us according to what we've given. It's largely because He changes our nature when He touches us, to the point that we actually produce the very thing we gave away. That is not to say any of it originates with us; all good gifts come from God. Period. But what a man sows, that shall he also reap. Some are too insecure to sow honor.

It is almost as though they think that they will be lacking if they give it away. Not so. All heavenly commodities increase as they are released. Those who show mercy have mercy returned to them. It's how this kingdom works.

Every time you bring encouragement to someone, you release divine favor.

Furthermore, shining is an act of *giving away who we are.* Yet who we are never diminishes. The light of God doesn't lessen the more we shine. It actually gets stronger. If we have received something from God, we shine as we give it away. It's the act of releasing internal realities and experiences that help to redefine the nature of the world we live in. Internal realities become external realities. That is the act of shining.

This is why we must discover this truth, "The kingdom of God is within you" (Luke 17:21, NKJV). I won't write a check if

I don't know that I have money in the bank. It is the discovery of the treasure that is in us through encountering the face of God that enables us to write checks that are consistent with His account, not ours. Peter said to the lame man, "Silver and gold have I none; but *such as I have give I thee*" (Acts 3:6, KJV, emphasis added). He then wrote a check that only God could back up. That is the way this kingdom works.

At one point Jesus invited all of humanity to come to Him and drink. "If anyone is thirsty, let him come to Me and drink.... 'From his innermost being will flow rivers of living water'" (John 7:37–38). The picture drawn by Jesus is once again very extreme. If I take a drink of refreshing from Him, a river of refreshing flows from me! A drink becomes a river. There is

If we have received something from God, we shine as we give it away.

an exponential increase in everything that God releases into our lives as we release it. It grows through use. The waters of refreshing that pour through us don't diminish as we give it away. The opposite is true. Our heartfelt capacity to give increases in the giving. What is seemingly small on the outside becomes eternally significant once it's on the inside—the kingdom within. Receiving grace from God defines the kind of grace we can distribute.

This river is actually the Holy Spirit Himself. He is in us as a river, not a lake. He's not merely with us to comfort us and abide in us. He is in us to flow through us to transform the nature of the world around us. This is what Peter released to the lame man at the gate. He gave what he had. In his survey of his inheritance in Christ, he discovered a river that can never run dry. It flows from the temple of God, getting deeper as it flows,[7] and works to change the course of world history—through you and me.

At some point we have to believe in the significance of God's touch in our lives. Many stand in line for prayers of impartation, week after week, hoping to finally get something powerful. It's noble to have such hunger to travel around the world in order to receive from great men and women of God. I do it and believe in it. But the frequency must not be tied to unbelief that God has not released what I've asked for in previous encounters. To keep us from being impartation junkies, He sometimes places His biggest impartation in something like *a time-release capsule*. It's a strange picture, but it is true. There are times where God touches us so significantly that it's effect has to be spread out over time, or it might distract us from His purposes. Our faith cannot depend merely on our *felt* experience. It must be on the promises of God.

RELEASING THE KINGDOM

Jesus is the Word of God made flesh. But when He spoke, the Word became Spirit. And that Spirit gave life.[8] This passage reveals one of the ways that the Spirit of God is released into a situation: through declaration.

When we follow the example that Jesus gave us and say only what the Father is saying, our words also become Spirit.

He is released into the environment as we speak. This concept is consistent with the whole of Scripture. "The kingdom of God is...in the Holy Spirit" (Romans 14:17). When the Holy Spirit is released into a situation, the King's dominion is manifested. The Spirit always works to demonstrate liberty and freedom,[9] which are signs that the King is present.

There is also a release of the Spirit through acts of faith. Faith so impressed Jesus that it caused Him to announce that certain stories of faith would be told throughout eternity, wherever His story is told. Realizing that faith brought about extraordinary miracles, and the miracles happened because of the Holy Spirit's work, it's not hard to see how the Holy Spirit is released through acts of faith. An act of faith is an action that is an evidence of the faith a person has. I have witnessed people who did not receive healing until they attempted to do what was impossible for them to do. The miracle was then released in the act.

Sometimes the Spirit of God is released through touch— more specifically, the laying on of hands.[10] The power of God dwells within a person.[11] Laying our hands on someone who is sick releases the power of God to destroy the affliction. When it's a proper place to touch, I like to lay my hand on the location of the disease or injury. I have felt tumors disappear under my hands. One woman had a tumor in her abdomen that was so large it was as if she was six months pregnant. I laid my hands on her abdomen and the tumor disappeared.

Perhaps the most unusual way to release the Spirit of God is through a prophetic act. This is where an action is taken in the natural that has nothing to do with the needed miracle. The prophet threw a stick in the water because a borrowed axe head fell into the bottom of the river. The axe head floated to the surface and was recovered.[12] There isn't a natural law that says that sticks in the water make iron float. Yet when it is an act that is directed by God, it will always release the Spirit of God to accomplish His purposes.

> *We give away what we have, and as we do, the world around us conforms. It is a superior kingdom.*

This particular manifestation is especially important for those who only like to do what they understand. God loves to address this weakness in us.

GIVING WHAT YOU HAVE

Jesus slept in a boat during a life-threatening storm. Some said it was because He was exhausted. I don't think so. The world He was dwelling in has no storms. Paul would later find language for Jesus's example saying that we live in "heavenly places in Christ."[13] Jesus lived from heaven toward Earth. That is the nature of faith. When it came time to stop the storm, He did so by releasing peace. He had it to give. Because His peace was authentic and was truly dwelling in Him, He could release it over the storm. And the storm was no match. Like Jesus, we have authority over any storm we can sleep in.

Through declaration His internal reality became His external reality. The peace that was ruling in Him soon became that which was released to rule around Him. That is the nature of the Christian life. We give away what we have, and as we do, the world around us conforms. It is a superior kingdom.

THE GLORY OF GOD BECOMES MANIFEST

The wonderful part of shining for God is that He backs it up. He literally shines through us when our glory is used for His, and our efforts are surrendered to His purposes. This is the role of co-laboring with Christ.

Let's look at an extended selection from Isaiah. Notice that God's glory is released as His crowning mark upon a people who shine as He assigned for them to do:

> Arise, shine; for your light has come,
> And the glory of the LORD has risen upon you.
> For behold, darkness will cover the earth
> And deep darkness the peoples;
> But the LORD will rise upon you
> And His glory will appear upon you.
> Nations will come to your light,
> And kings to the brightness of your rising.
> Lift up your eyes round about and see;

They all gather together, they come to you.

Your sons will come from afar,

And your daughters will be carried in the arms.

Then you will see and be radiant,

And your heart will thrill and rejoice;

Because the abundance of the sea will be turned to you,

The wealth of the nations will come to you.

—ISAIAH 60:1–5

Through this prophetic promise God provides specific instruction about our approach to life and what kind of results He is looking for through that approach. We are to live intentionally, knowing the kind of impact we are to have even before we see it for ourselves. The ramifications of this prophetic word go far beyond most of our hopes, dreams, and visions. Isaiah declared entire nations and their leaders would be transformed. We'd then see the wealth of the nations released to the church for kingdom purposes. But all the fruit and breakthrough provided in these promises are connected to one thing—the manifest presence of God upon His people. It's the manifestation of His glory.

Herein lies the challenge—we are commanded to arise and shine in the midst of deep, depressing darkness that covers those around us. God responds to our obedience by releasing His glory. Our shining attracts His glory! And it's His glory released that brings about the greatest transformation in lives, cities, and nations.

We once had a spontaneous prophetic song (a song of the Lord) in which the Lord said, "Did I not fill the tabernacle of Moses with My glory? Did I not fill the temple of Solomon with

My glory? How much more will I fill the place that I build with My own hands? My beloved, I am building you!"

The hands of man built every house of God in the Bible. God always helped by giving the instructions on how it was to be constructed. But God Himself is actually building the church as His eternal dwelling place. If He filled the houses He didn't build with His glory, how much more will He fill the one He is building? It's not right to put that event off into the future after Jesus returns. It has to be now. Some words have power for any generation that will take responsibility for them. How do we know this is for now? Because in the Scripture it occurs when deep darkness is on people. It describes a time like now. Furthermore, the release of His glory is promised to the group of people who have the capacity to arise and shine with divine purpose. This can only happen to the people to whom the light of God has come. We are that people, and Jesus Christ, our light, has come.

If you've spent time in the Old Testament, you're probably familiar with how dramatically God displayed His presence in the houses built for Him by men. Studying these events should help put God's promise to fill His church into an even better context for you. We must remember that inferior covenants cannot provide superior blessings. For example, because it is in Scripture, we often take for granted the things that were released to Israel in the wilderness on their way to the land of promises, not only the miracles of provision and victories in battle but also the abiding presence of God in the cloud and the fire. They weren't born again, they were living in rebellion, and yet God was seen among them. That all happened under an inferior covenant. We need to look at these things and ask, "If He did that for them, how much more will He do for us?"

LOOKING IN A MIRROR

The glory of God ought to be seen upon His people. It makes little difference to me whether it is a physical manifestation that is seen by the natural eye or it is something that people perceive through the eyes of their hearts.

There is an unusual lesson found in the third chapter of 2 Corinthians. The apostle Paul is discussing Moses's experience with the glory of God and how Israel insisted that he put a veil over his face because the glory frightened them. Paul then says, "The veil is taken away in Christ" (2 Corinthians 3:14, NKJV). That means that whatever was hidden under the veil is now available for all to see. The fear element that Israel struggled with has been removed because the Spirit of Christ has come to make us free.

> Now the Lord is the Spirit, and where the Spirit of the Lord is, there is liberty. But we all, with unveiled face, beholding as in a mirror the glory of the Lord, are being transformed into the same image from glory to glory, just as by the Spirit of the Lord.
>
> —2 CORINTHIANS 3:17–18, NKJV

The freedom that the Holy Spirit brings releases us to behold the glory! And strangely, that glory is seen as though we were looking in a mirror. In other words, that is what we look like. That is what the Holy Spirit's job has been—to make us glorious. "That He might present to Himself the church in all her glory, having no spot or wrinkle or any such thing; but that she would be holy and blameless" (Ephesians 5:27). Jesus is returning for a bride whose body is in equal proportion to her head. The command to *arise and shine* is the process through which we are able to step into the reality of who God says we already are.

REDISCOVERING OUR MESSAGE

I can threaten people with hell and have a measure of breakthrough in getting converts. Hell is real and must not be ignored. But that is not plan A. It is plan B. Plan A is, "The kindness of God leads you to repentance" (Romans 2:4). This truth must affect our attitude. When this concept affects our approach to humanity we are much more likely use our favor to serve them effectively, which better represents life in the kingdom.[14]

We are entering a period of time where we will see more and more people coming to Christ because of His face shining upon the people of God. Sometimes it will be His raw power that manifests through us, and other times it will be His selfless love with works of kindness. But His face will be seen, as it must.

The face of God will be encountered over and over again. It is shining on the church right now. It is time to see and be enlarged, for it changes our capacity to represent Him in this world as it changes the nature of who we are. We tend to manifest His likeness in equal measure to how deep our encounters have been.

A fear of God is about to come upon the church. We've experienced it at times because of trial and discipline. But there is something that is about to overtake the people of God that comes from a revelation of His kindness. This kind of blessing does not promote arrogance. On the contrary: there's such an overwhelming sense of His goodness that we are undone. We will become a trembling group of people because we consciously live so far beyond what we deserve. This is not to imply that problems and conflict will be gone. It just means that for the first time in history those problems will consistently yield to a church with authority. It is the contrast that is spoken of in Isaiah 60—darkness covers the earth, but His glory is upon His people. That realization will provoke us to fear God in a new way that ultimately stirs up the nations around us to come to Christ. We become the "city set on a hill" (Matthew 5:14). There is a realm of the blessing in God that has not yet been experienced. And it is the Lord's intent to release this upon His people before the end comes. This blessing enables us to function more like brokers of His world rather than beggars for His invasion.

Psalm 67 captures this prophetic picture of God's heart for His people as the method He would like to use to reach the nations. We can be groomed by His Spirit through divine encounters to be qualified to carry such a responsibility. The face of His favor is available for those who are desperate. He longs for us to be able to carry His likeness into any setting. His blessing upon us will bring the fear of God back to the nations. Let's become candidates for this mandate by embracing the quest for face-to-face encounters with God. The time is now.

> God be merciful to us and bless us,
> And cause His face to shine upon us.
> That Your way may be known on earth,
> Your salvation among all nations.
> Let the peoples praise You, O God;
> Let all the peoples praise You.
> Oh, let the nations be glad and sing for joy!
> For You shall judge the people righteously,
> And govern the nations on earth.
> Let the peoples praise You, O God;
> Let all the peoples praise You.
> Then the earth shall yield her increase;
> God, our own God, shall bless us.
> God shall bless us,
> And all the ends of the earth shall fear Him.
>
> —PSALM 67:1–7, NKJV

NOTES

CHAPTER 1
THE JOURNEY BEGINS

1. I define religion as "form without power." As such, it always disappoints.

2. Proverbs 14:4.

CHAPTER 2
THE FAVOR OF HIS FACE

1. Psalm 8:3.

2. Mark 8:15.

CHAPTER 3
HEADING TO THE PROMISED LAND

1. 2 Corinthians 7:10.

2 Malachi 2:15.

3. Romans 8:28.

4. 1 Corinthians 10:2.

5. John 15:3.

6.   The denominational spirit is divisive in nature. Denominations are not the problem, but rather the hearts of God's people; many of those who are a part of denominations are free from that influence, and many outside of denominations are bound by it.

7.   Isaiah 28:10.

CHAPTER 4
HIS MANIFEST PRESENCE

1.   Acts 2:16–17.

2.   John 2.

3.   Matthew 28:19.

4.   Ephesians 1:13–14; Romans 8:11, 15.

5.   Ephesians 5:18.

6.   1 Corinthians 4:20.

7.   Exodus 33:1–4.

CHAPTER 5
JESUS: THE FACE OF GOD

1.   Luke 1:41–45.

2.   Luke 1:20, 59–64.

3.   Matthew 3:11.

4.   Matthew 10:8.

5.   John 1:14.

6.   Exodus 33:18–19.

CHAPTER 6
SETTING UP AN AMBUSH

1. Luke 10:38–42.

2. Matthew 9:21.

3. This was probably the Lord Himself.

4. Romans 3:23.

CHAPTER 7
NEVER THE SAME AGAIN

1. Richard M. Riss, *A Survey of 20th Century Revival Movements in North America* (Peabody, MA: Hendrickson Publishers, 1988), 32.

2. Gordon Lindsay, ed., *The John G. Lake Sermons on Dominion Over Demons, Disease, and Death* (Olendale, CA: The Bhurrh Press: Farson and Sons, 1949), 5–9, used by permission of Christ For The Nations, Inc., Dallas, TX.

3. Ibid.

4. Ibid.

5. Ibid.

6. Teresa A. Taylor, "Jesus the Healer," *Healing and Revival Press*, HealingRevival.com, http://www.healingandrevival.com/BioJGLake.htm (accessed June 21, 2007).

7. Ibid.

8. Charles G. Finney, *Memoirs of Rev. Charles G. Finney* (New York: A. S. Barnes & Company, 1896), 19–23.

9. Ibid., 183–184.

10. John Crowder, *Miracle Workers, Reformers, and the New Mystics* (Shippensburg, PA: Destiny Image, 2006), 264–265.

11. Stanley Howard Frodsham, *Smith Wigglesworth: Apostle of Faith* (Springfield, MO: Gospel Publishing House, 1948), 44.

12. Diana Chapman, *Searching the Source of the River: Forgotten Women of the Pentecostal Revival in Britain 1907–1914* (London: PUSH Publishing, 2007), 153–154.

13. Ibid.

14. H. V. Roberts, *New Zealand's Greatest Revival; Reprint of the 1922 Revival Classic: Smith Wigglesworth* (Dilsburg, PA: Rex Burgher Books [www.klifemin.org], 1951), 46–47.

15. Teresa A. Taylor, "Apostle of Faith," *Healing and Revival Press*, HealingRevival.com, http://www.healingandrevival.com/BioSWigglesworth.htm (accessed June 21, 2007).

16. Ibid.

17. Ibid.

18. T. L. Osborn. *Healing the Sick: A Living Classic* (Tulsa, OK: Harrison House Publisher, 1986), 276–281, 328.

19. Ibid.

20. Rolland and Heidi Baker, *There Is Always Enough: The Story of Rolland and Heidi Baker's Miraculous Ministry Among the Poor* (Tonbridge, England: Sovereign World Ltd., 2003), 67–70.

21. Ibid.

22. Ibid.

23. Ibid.

24   Bill Johnson, *Dreaming With God* (Shippensburg, PA: Destiny Image Publishing, 2006), 179–180. These two paragraphs are from that book.

CHAPTER 8
JOY: THE REWARD

1.   Luke 2:10.

2.   Isaiah 53:4–5.

3.   Colossians 1:24. The word for *affliction* in this verse is not sickness. It means *to put under pressure*, as when grapes are crushed for wine or olives for olive oil. Righteous living puts us under pressures that bring out the inward anointing and joy of the Holy Spirit.

4.   Acts 4:28–29.

5.   Deuteronomy 6:17.

6.   Psalm 111:2.

7.   2 Corinthians 2:11.

8   James G. Friesen, PhD, et al., *The Life Model: Living From the Heart Jesus Gave You* (Pasadena, CA: Shepherd's House, Inc., 2000), 11.

CHAPTER 9
REFLECTION OF THE FACE OF GOD

1.   2 Corinthians 5:17.

2.   Psalm 102:18; 1 Peter 2:9.

3.   John 9:1–4; 14:12.

4.   John 5:1–8.

5.   1 John 4:19.

6. Luke 10:33.

7. Romans 14:17.

8. Malachi 4:2.

9. My book *Dreaming With God* deals with this subject at length.

10. Haggai 2:7, NKJV.

11. Matthew 5:5; 1 Corinthians 3:22.

12. Proverbs 8:22–31.

13. 1 Kings 10:4–5.

14 See www.TheCall.com.

CHAPTER 10
A PEOPLE OF HIS GLORY

1. 2 Corinthians 3:7.

2. *Mountain* is a metaphorical term used to describe our ascending into His presence; see Psalm 24:3.

3. 2 Corinthians 5:21.

4. 1 John 4:20.

5. 1 Corinthians 15:39–41.

6. Proverbs 18:21.

7. Ezekiel 47.

8. John 6:63.

9. 2 Corinthians 3:17.

10. Hebrews 6:2.

11. Mark 5:30.

12. 2 Kings 6:5–6.

13. Ephesians 1:3.

14. Matthew 20:26–28.